58

Critical Guides to French Texts

88 Rabelais: Pantagruel *and* Gargantua

Critical Guides to French Texts

EDITED BY ROGER LITTLE, WOLFGANG VAN EMDEN,
DAVID WILLIAMS

RABELAIS

Pantagruel *and* Gargantua

Kathleen M. Hall

formerly Senior Lecturer in French,
University of Southampton

Grant & Cutler Ltd
1991

ISBN 0 7293 0328 4

I.S.B.N. 84-599-3256-7

DEPÓSITO LEGAL: V. 2.846 - 1991

Printed in Spain by
Artes Gráficas Soler, S.A., Valencia
for
GRANT & CUTLER LTD
55-57 GREAT MARLBOROUGH STREET, LONDON W1V 2AY

Contents

Prefatory Note

A critical guide to Rabelais must inevitably also be a guide to critical work on him. Almost every comment made on him is bound to be controversial; but it is hoped that this book will at least serve as a signpost to or through some of the controversies. Non-specialists may go into as many or as few as they wish.

The text used, for convenience, is that of *Rabelais, Œuvres complètes*, ed. Pierre Jourda, Paris (Garnier), 1962 (Bibliography, *2*). The Select Bibliography lists other abbreviations used here. Capitalization in sixteenth-century titles follows house style.

It should be noted that what makes up *Pantagruel* chapters 10-13 in Jourda's and most editions was a single chapter before 1534, and was wrongly numbered as a second ch.9 in the original, re-edited as *François Rabelais, Pantagruel* by V.-L. Saulnier in 1959 (Bibliography, *3*). *3* numbers this chapter 9 *bis*; 2's ch. 14 is therefore *3*'s ch. 10, 2's ch. 15 is *3*'s ch. 11.

2's 16-17 form a single ch. 12 in the original and in *3*; 2's 18-20 a single ch. 13; 2's 21-22 a ch. 14; 2's 23-24 a ch. 15 and 2's 25-26 a ch. 16.

2's 27 is *3*'s 17, and so on to 2's 33-34, a single ch. 23 in the original and in *3*.

Editions of *Gargantua* before 1542 treated as single chapters what then became its chapters 4-5 and 21-22. This results in a similar though slighter *décalage* between *2* and the *Textes Littéraires Français* edition, *4*.

1. Introduction: The Prologues

The first thing always to be remembered when reading Rabelais is that he intends to amuse. Much more lies behind his joking, but he is an entertainer first and foremost. In a piece of verse which, conforming to a widespread publishing convention of the time, introduces the *Gargantua*, he quotes Aristotle to the effect that laughter is the distinguishing mark of man. (On this side of Rabelais see especially *8, 15 , 16, 25, 30, 38,* or *46*.)

It is hard for a critic, hard even for Rabelais himself, to communicate through the printed word alone this intention and this power of entertaining. A comedian's performance relies not only on words but on vocal effects, varied laughs and smiles, timing and surprise, presence and charisma. Printing supplies a mere record of the words; but it has the advantage that the reader can turn back, re-read, see passages in juxtaposition and as a whole. Once the explanation of an old word or a puzzling detail in Rabelais's text, of a subtle approach or an unexpected allusion has elicited a mental chuckle at its suddenly realized aptness, one must re-read the passage as if hearing it for the first time, accompanied by Rabelais's deeper chuckle, full of understanding and carrying one with it. Rabelais has had a permanent influence on French humour and prose style; he has also contributed much to French thought with its characteristic clarity and precision, enriching it by striking sayings and symbols.

Knowledge of who he was and what was his background will help towards an understanding of what he is saying, how and why. He was born in the pleasant Loire valley towards the end of the fifteenth century, about 1483 according to Saulnier (*3*), Screech (*41*) and Demerson (*21*); about 1494 according to Jourda (*2*), Plattard (*35*) and Villey (*48*); the earlier date fits better with Dupèbe's

evidence (*BHR*, XLII (1980), p.657 and *ER*, XVIII (1985), p.175).
Whether we are to picture Rabelais as not yet forty or as passing
fifty in the early 1530s can make a difference to our picture of him at
that time.

The 1530s in France could not be called a period of civil
dissension such as the country was to see in the second half of the
century (let alone other countries in this century), but it was a time
when belonging to the wrong religious party could have more
serious consequences than belonging to the wrong political one in
modern Britain, and when the *Parlement* or the *prévôté* of Paris
could order a search for prohibited religious books like a modern
search for prohibited drugs. Countering the gradual and scattered
advances of Reformed thinking, the *Parlement* had in August 1521
ordered the surrender of works by Luther and other heretical books,
and followed up the order by searches and arrests. In August 1523
Brother Jean Vallière was burnt to death on a charge of blasphemy;
J. Viénot (*Histoire de la Réforme française des origines à l'Édit de
Nantes*, Paris, 1926) counts four similar executions in 1525, and
others every year to 1530. In October 1534 a night-time outbreak of
anti-Catholic fly-posting in Paris and elsewhere, and in January 1535
a scattering of pamphlets taking a similar line, were to panic the
government into more executions and a temporary ban on all printing, throughout the country, on any subject.[1]

There is no doubt of Rabelais's dyed-in-the-wool royalism; his
religious views have always been a subject of much more controversy. Trained as a monk (or, more precisely, a Franciscan friar) he
acquired a wide education, extending to the new humanist learning
of the Renaissance, law and medicine; details of his biography are
given especially fully by Plattard (*35*), Lote (*33*) and Antonioli (*6*).
By 1532 he had been secretary to the local bishop, had moved in
literary circles in cathedral cities, had gained university degrees, and
had finally taken to life in the outside world as a practising doctor in

---

[1]See the *New Cambridge Modern History*, II, *The Reformation*, ed. G.R.
Elton, Cambridge University Press, 1958, especially chapters I and VI.3; for
more details on the *affaires des placards*, G. Berthoud, *Antoine Marcourt*,
Geneva (Droz), 1973, especially pp.171-89.

Lyons. He took care to regularize his ecclesiastical position in 1536, by obtaining absolution from the Pope for his 'apostasy', his leaving his monastery and abandoning the life of a monk, and by obtaining a transfer to another monastery which was about to be secularized, transformed into a collegiate church with dean and canons but without prior, abbot or monks. In Lyons he helped a firm of printers, being responsible for bringing out in 1532 editions of two medical books, firstly the letters of an Italian physician, Manardi, and secondly an anthology of works by the ancient doctors Hippocrates and Galen.

This factual account abounds in implications and puzzles. It could be the story of a lax Catholic, with wider interests than a monastic career permitted, who took every opportunity to bend the regulations of his order without actually breaking them. It could be the story of a man open to the thinking of the Reforming movements of the time, movements either within the Catholic Church (see A. Renaudet, *Préréforme et humanisme à Paris pendant les premières guerres d'Italie*, Paris, 1916), or rejecting it or rejected by it; or of a man open to the free-thinking rationalist ideas whose gradual penetration into France is traced by Busson (*13*). Whichever of these three types best reflects Rabelais, or whether he combined any two or all three, a man with such a lively and inquiring mind as his could in his age well have taken orders, less from unworldly piety than in the hope of finding a good education and congenial company among intellectual equals. His subsequent moves could have sprung from mental as much as moral dissatisfaction; and his 1536 manoeuvres, whatever his private views, could have been inspired by prudence during that period of intensifying religious divisions and crises. We shall come back to these questions.

Rabelais has been made world-famous, however, by his works of comic fiction, *Pantagruel*, *Gargantua* and their sequels. (Readers should beware of references to *Gargantua* as Book I and *Pantagruel* as Book II, arising either because that is their order in Rabelais's story, or because early critics thought that to have been their order of composition.)

The first edition of *Pantagruel* is undated; for Lefranc (*1*), Jourda (*2*), Plattard (*35*) and Saulnier (*3*) the date was November 1532; for Villey (*48*) possibly August 1532; for Screech (*ER*, XV (1980)) perhaps late autumn or (more probably) winter 1531, certainly before 26 March 1533; for Françon (*Studi Francesi*, L (1973), pp.276-82) April 1533. The title-page of the first edition of *Gargantua* is missing; Screech (*4*, pp.xl-xlv, and *ER*, XI, pp.9-55), Françon (*ER*, XI, pp.81-82) and Mireille Huchon (*ER*, XVI, pp.111-13) admit that it could have been as early as January 1534, but would like to think it after the *placards*, as late as February 1535 or even June 1535. So there might have been as short an interval as nine months between the two books (though this is unlikely) or as long as three-and-a-half years. The *Tiers Livre des faictz ... du noble Pantagruel* appeared in 1546, the *Quart Livre* in part in 1548 and in full in 1552. The argument as to whether the posthumous *Cinquiesme Livre* is genuinely by Rabelais still continues (see chapter 8 below).

These books present in their prologues, parenthetical comments and some whole chapters an authorial persona which may or may not reflect Rabelais's own personality.[2] Rabelais wears his enormous learning lightly, quoting impressive references but concealing the real ones,[3] and mixing them with everyday proverbs, allusions, puns and expletives. He presents himself as a friendly fellow, interested primarily in drink, sex and cheap light literature; in the opening apostrophe of *Pantagruel*, 'Très illustres et très chevaleureux champions, gentilz homes et aultres', the archaism 'champions' indicates that 'gentilz' also is an undeserved conventional compliment and that the actual address is to the 'aultres', who will become the 'Beuveurs tres illustres, et vous, Verolez tres precieux' of the opening apostrophe of *Gargantua* ('vérole' being

---

[2] See especially *16*, chs. 3 and 4; *26*, pp.13-36 and 64-65; *45*, *passim*; and R.C. Cholakian, *The 'moi' in the middle distance: a study of the narrative voice in Rabelais*, Madrid (Porrúa Turanzas), 1982.

[3] e.g., the opening of the Prologue to *Gargantua* (about 250 words), which cites Plato, is in fact expanded from Erasmus, *Adagia*, III iii 1. Readers of Erasmus in Rabelais's time might remember how he goes on: '... is not Christ the most extraordinary Silenus of all?' (Tr. by M.M. Phillips, *The 'Adages' of Erasmus*, Cambridge, 1964, p.271.)

venereal disease. On Rabelais's 'obscenity', see p.19 below. The theme of wine and its inspiring effects runs throughout Rabelais's books; see, e.g., T.M. Greene in *RIB* and A. Gendre in *ER*, XXI.) Rabelais's public, in reality, would be the small proportion of the population who could read or arrange to be read aloud to. Among them, the more cultured ones would be fully able to appreciate his subtler allusions, though it is only rarely that either his humour or his thought depends wholly on such allusions.

His style is essentially oral. In centuries when Latin was the language of serious writing and discussion, it was spoken in the schools from the lowest forms; Rabelais would have been educated as much by listening and replying orally in Latin as by reading and writing. But Franciscan friars used French too; he would have been trained as a preacher in the popular style to those who knew no Latin (see especially *28*, pp.61-90). Outdoors, he would have been entertained by open-air theatre, showmen and salesmen, and indoors, when long dark evenings had to be whiled away, by the talkers and story-tellers among whom he was to become chief. He talks with colloquialisms, exclamations, hyperboles, and an apparently irrepressible fountain of words which yet produces carefully calculated structures: a striking opening, an unexpected development, phrase piled on phrase, clause on clause to preposterous heights, at the climax swerving aside into a new and surprising direction, and suddenly subsiding into anticlimax: 'if you don't believe me, so much the worse for you' (*Pantagruel*, 1, eds of 1534 and 1542, last lines, and *Gargantua*, 6, last lines, freely translated).[4]

What Rabelais tells, ostensibly just re-telling but in reality wholly transforming it, is a story which was circulating in France in various forms, that of the giant Gargantua. It may have come down orally from folklore (see especially *1*, I, pp.xxviii-xxxvi; *31*, pp.141-81; and H. Dontenville, *La France mythologique*, Nancy, 1966; but also *45*, *passim*). By Rabelais's time it was appearing in little chapbooks, the equivalent of the modern science-fiction paperback.

---

[4] If a structuralist or post-structuralist approach to Rabelais's art is desired, the most helpful are perhaps those of Glauser, *25*, Gray, *26*, and La Charité, *30*.

Seven survive, some in more than one copy, and four have been
republished, most recently in *Les Chroniques gargantuines*, ed.
C. Lauvergnat-Gagnière, G. Demerson and others, Paris (Nizet),
1988: *La Grande et Merveilleuse Vie du trespuissant et redoubté
Roy de Gargantua ...*, *Les Grandes et Inestimables Cronicques: du
grant et enorme geant Gargantua ...*, *Le Vroy Gargantua* and *Les
Croniques admirables du puissant roy Gargantua*. (On all, see
Lewis, *32*; it is doubtful how much Rabelais knew about early
medieval epic or romance.)

Set in the time of a nursery-tale King Arthur, the chapbooks
turn on thrills and broad humour, sometimes introduced with a
parody of pedantry:

> Pour le commencement de ceste vraye cronique vous
> devez scavoir comme tesmoigne l'escripture de plusieurs
> Cronicqueurs, dont nous en laisserons aulchuns, comme
> Gaguin, André, maistre Jehan Lemaire et aultres
> semblables, lesquelz ne servent rien a propos quant a
> ceste presente histoire: mais prandrons ... Lancelot du
> Lac, et tous les chevaliers de la Table Ronde, et aultres
> semblables, dont en y a assez pour approuver la verité de
> ceste presente histoire ... (*Le Vroy Gargantua*, 1)

Gargantua is born of a gigantic father and mother made by Merlin to
help King Arthur, destroys enemy armies with an iron club, and is
finally carried away to live with Arthur in the castle of Avallon in
Fairyland. Rabelais may have contributed three chapters (*Pantagruel*
2-4, with part of 5) to one of these chapbooks, *Les Croniques
admirables* (the view of M. Huchon, *ER*, XVI (1981), p.399), or it
may have stolen three chapters of his (the view of Lefranc and
Jourda, *1*, I, p.xlv and 2, p.232); the view that he copied from it is
that of Françon (*Le Vroy Gargantua*, ed. M. Françon, Paris, 1949,
pp.123-25) but is unlikely.

The hero of Rabelais's first published volume of fiction is not
Gargantua himself but his giant son Pantagruel, given a brief
mention in only two of the chapbooks, perhaps under Rabelais's

influence, and better known as a thirst-provoking imp (see *1*, III, pp.xv-xxiii). Pantagruel's adventures are roughly based by Rabelais on those of the popular Gargantua; we hear similarly of his wonderful birth, his exploits in childhood, in Paris and in war, and his final triumph; but it is his intellectual reactions and development which diverge from the folk-narrative and make him into a figure symbolizing what seemed to Rabelais the best of the Renaissance. (The question of the extent to which the Pantagruel and Gargantua of Rabelais are comic figures will be treated in later chapters here, particularly 4.)

In the next two years Rabelais produced his second volume, a further re-working simultaneously of the chapbook story of Gargantua and of his own story of Pantagruel. The fantasy remains, but Gargantua's mental and moral development is traced in a more linear and more detailed fashion, making him into a worthy and credible father of the hero Pantagruel has now developed into. Gargantua mirrors in his long life the gradual coming of the French Renaissance, as Pantagruel mirrors its achievements by the 1530s. In the two years or so between the books, Rabelais himself matured considerably; many readers find more shrewdness and wisdom in *Gargantua* than in *Pantagruel*, and a richer and more satisfying texture. But Rabelais's imaginative capacities and humour are equal in the two books; *Pantagruel*, as both Defaux and La Charité find (*18*, p.208, and *30*, p.18), is different rather than inferior.

The introduction to *Le Vroy Gargantua* has been quoted above almost in full; the only extant *Gargantua* which we can be sure was published before *Pantagruel*, *Les Grandes et Inestimables Cronicques*, opens with only the brief salutation: ' Tous bons chevaliers et gentilz hommes vous debves scavoir ...' But Rabelais provides *Pantagruel* with a separate and extensive prologue, a parodic reproduction of a piece of salesman's patter. The first three-quarters advertise *Les Grandes et Inestimables Cronicques*, evidently known to Rabelais at first hand, as being full of profitable fruit and a remedy for all troubles; the last quarter surprises by using that buildup to advertise 'un aultre livre de mesme billon, sinon qu'il est un peu plus equitable et digne de foy'. The basis of *Pantagruel* is personal knowledge, Rabelais assures us, although with tell-tale exaggerations, 'j'en parle comme sainct Jehan de l'Apocalypse' (2, p.218, editions before 1542), and pretended slips of the tongue, 'Onocrotale, voyre dy je, crotenotaire', meaning to say *protonotaire*; and, in mock sincerity and fury, he invokes a horrible fate for himself if he is lying, and a parallel fate for readers who disbelieve him. (See Gray in *RIB*.)

The Prologue to *Gargantua* is not a re-working of the Prologue to *Pantagruel* but a new composition, a parody of a dedication with suitably humble praise of a patron or patrons — in this case, the 'Beuveurs... et ...Verolez' — requests for 'benevolence' and tactful insinuations of the value of the work presented.[5] There have been innumerable studies of this Prologue's ambiguities. The first two-thirds of the Prologue warn the reader not to be misled by appearances but to stand by for a hidden

> sustantificque mouelle ... et doctrine plus absconce,
> laquelle vous revelera de très haultz sacremens et
> mysteres horrificques, tant en ce qui concerne nostre
> religion que aussi l'estat politicq et vie oeconomique.
>
> (2, p.8)

In the last third Rabelais suddenly swings round: the allegorical senses of the Iliad and the Odyssey, he says, were never conceived of by Homer — they have been read into the epics by foolish commentators — but if you agree with him on this, why should you not 'do the same' with his book, 'pourquoy autant n'en ferez de ces joyeuses et nouvelles chronicques ...?'

Does this mean that we should read into Rabelais's work allegorical meanings, conscious or unconscious, or that we would

---

[5] See especially, in chronological order, Spitzer, *44*, pp.406-09; J. Paris, *Rabelais au futur*, Paris, 1970, pp.11-47; Coleman, *16*, pp.31-36; A. Gendre, 'Le prologue de "Pantagruel", le prologue de "Gargantua", examen comparatif', *Revue d'hist. litt. de la France*, LXXIV (1974), pp.3-19; Gray, *26*, pp.13-22; Vachon, *47*, pp.59-66; Screech, *41*, pp.124-30; Duval, *22*; and Stephens, *45*, pp.280-89.

read them in foolishly and should rather believe there are none? Rabelais deliberately leaves his readers in a state of complete confusion, only asking them to read on and credit him with meaning well: 'interpretez tous mes faictz et mes dictz en la perfectissime partie ... et guayement lisez le reste ...' (2, p.9). 'Over the course of the prologue', Duval explains, the reader is asked to 'look beyond the frivolous titles ... beyond the frivolous literal meaning ...', beyond even 'the frivolous inspiration of the book ... The "benevolence" being sought is no longer ... a simple predisposition on the part of the reader to be persuaded by the writer's arguments ... Benevolence has been transformed into a positive virtue to be cultivated for its own sake in the hearts and minds of all readers' (op.cit., pp.12 and 14). We shall see that this emphasis on 'benevolence' recurs elsewhere in the books of Rabelais, 'played out on an epic scale', as Duval concludes.

Rabelais's comic techniques as used in his Prologues can be discerned in miniature even in his title-pages and their variants — for, over the years, Rabelais revised his works several times for republication, with alterations and improvements which it is always interesting, often informative and sometimes important to study. The title-page of *Les Grandes et Inestimables Cronicques* runs in full:

> Les grandes et inestimables Cronicques du grant et enorme geant Gargantua: Contenant sa genealogie, la grandeur et force de son corps. Aussi ses merveilleux faictz d'armes qu'il fist pour le Roy Artus, comme verrez cy apres. Imprimé nouvellement. 1532.

Rabelais evidently used that as a model for the original title-page of *Pantagruel*:

> Pantagruel. Les horribles et espouventables faictz et prouesses du tresrenommé Pantagruel Roy des Dipsodes, filz du grant geant Gargantua, composez nouvellement par maistre Alcofrybas Nasier ...

Rabelais has intensified the adjectives, stressed the hero's ancestry, elevated him to a throne, and masked himself with an anagram of his own name, meaningless to the general public though decipherable by his friends. In the 1534 edition he further equips himself with a Greek motto, less esoteric than it seems, ΑΓΑΘΗ ΤΥΧΗ, 'good luck to it', and with a pretentious title, 'abstracteur de quinte essence', chemist who transmutes base metals into gold and distils the secret elixir of life. The same Greek motto and title appear on the first extant title-page of *Gargantua*:

> Gargantua. ΑΓΑΘΗ ΤΥΧΗ. La vie inestimable du grand Gargantua, pere de Pantagruel, jadis composee par L'abstracteur de quinte essence, livre plein de pantagruelisme ... 1535.

The word 'inestimable' is picked up from the *Cronicques*, but the emphasis is on the family relationship, making the page serve as an advertisement both for *Pantagruel* and for *Gargantua*.

The important 1542 edition of both books was revised by Rabelais with an eye on ultra-Catholic censors, particularly the Faculty of Theology at the Sorbonne (see p.34 below); neither book had yet incurred any formal ecclesiastical condemnation (see 23, pp.105-32), but the general climate called for even more caution than a decade before. The title-page of *Pantagruel* describes him as 'restitué à son naturel', perhaps to indicate that this is to be taken as the only authentic version. The life of Gargantua becomes 'très horrificque', perhaps to stress its quality of fantasy. The pseudonym of Rabelais is reduced to 'Alcofribas' in both texts, so that the anagram and the joke are comprehensible only to those who know earlier editions of *Pantagruel*.

However, in all editions authorized by Rabelais, *Gargantua* is a 'livre plein de pantagruelisme'. We shall see in later chapters what is meant by this.

2. The Hero's Birth: Pantagruel 1-3 and Gargantua 1-6

In the centuries before the neo-classical opening *in medias res*, it was usual to start a narrative at the beginning, and to support the hero's claim to fame by emphasis on the good fortune of his birth and the merits of his ancestry, traced as far back as the narrator pleased. The Gargantua of *Les Grandes et Inestimables Cronicques* was a giant by reason of his birth to giant parents, who had been created intentionally by Merlin's magic from the bones of whales, Lancelot's blood and Guenevere's nail-parings, so that the son of such giants might be able to defend King Arthur against all enemies. The story, to the moment of the hero's birth, extends to over one-fifth of the *Cronicques*. This narrative element occupies a smaller proportion of Rabelais's two much longer books; yet he treats it generously, in three chapters of *Pantagruel* and six of *Gargantua*. *Pantagruel* 1 traces the genealogy back with deliberate absurdity to a race of giants that originated accidentally, during the generation after Adam, from eating outsize medlars.

In these opening chapters of both books Rabelais's aim is almost solely to amuse. The first 180 words or so of the first and rather shorter edition of *Pantagruel* are a glorious string of hits at the use of Biblical commonplaces by other writers ('peu après que Abel fust occis par son frere Caïn'), of banal rhyming ('tous fruictz qui ... nous sont produytz'), of exaggerations ('grosses mesles, car les troys en faisoyent le boysseau'), of impossibilities ('la sepmaine des troys jeudis'), of so-called precision ('moys de octobre, ce me semble, ou bien de septembre (affin que je ne erre)') and of so-called science ('car il y en eut troys, à cause des irreguliers bissextes ...') (2, pp.221-22). Later editions progressively enrich the passage: in 1533 Rabelais adds the chatty phrase 'veu que sommes de sejour', in 1534 'le soleil bruncha quelque peu'. In 1537 he continues this phrase,

'comme *debitoribus*, à gauche', and, though he cuts out a risky reference to 'les auteurs de la saincte Escripture comme monseigneur
sainct Luc et sainct Matthieu', he replaces them by the 'Gregoys,
Gentilz, qui furent buveurs eternels'. In 1542 he adds '(je parle de
loing, il y a plus de quarante quarantaines de nuyctz, pour nombrer à
la mode des antiques Druides)', the two lines on the (non-existent)
Greek Kalends, Lent and 'la my oust', the rest of the parenthesis after
'je ne erre', and all the mock-pedantic passage from 'et feut
manifestement veu ...' to the point where he explodes its pretensions:
'aussy auroient ils les dens bien longues s'ilz povoient toucher
jusques là.'

On the pegs of the two correct Genesis references, that to Abel
already noticed and that to Noah which soon follows, the rest of the
chapter hangs a fantastic legend supported similarly by topical and
literary allusions, Latin tags, emphatic enumerations and compar-
isons, and a final dash of scepticism in the shape of the 1534
addition: 'car, si ne le croiez, non foys je, fist elle' (2, p.228; see p.11
above, *11*, I, pp.27-29, and *45*, pp.195-96 and 215-52).

Chapter 2 gives a similarly fanciful description of the drought
when Pantagruel was born, so contrived as to culminate in a mock-
etymology of his name.[6] The pseudo-Biblical etymologies (an
example of the device of pseudo-reference to irrelevant authorities
noticed above, p.12) and the details indicating the giant's size seem
to be the only comic devices which these three chapters of
Pantagruel inherit from *Les Grandes et Inestimables Cronicques*;
but Rabelais takes the devices much further. The pseudo-references
become lengthier, more recondite and more precise, like the hundred
or so words allegedly from 'le Philosophe' Empedocles (2, pp.229-
30; see *ER*, XXI (1988), pp.394-96); the detail of the twelve stags
killed by Grandgousier and slung round his neck in the *Cronicques*
may have inspired Rabelais to create the far more outrageous
procession which issues from Badebec's womb. He has many other
humorous resources, painting now, *à la* Bosch, the panorama of a

---

[6] Critics argue rather pointlessly whether this picture of drought is a reference to an exceptional one in 1532; Screech, *41*, p.37, sums up: there was
drought in France from 1528 to 1534.

whole continent stricken by drought, complete with screaming fish; now, *à la* Breughel, a crowd of church-goers exhausting the supply of holy water and, under the control of a Papal regulation, queuing up for the last drops. A dominant device in chapter 2 is the use of sharply juxtaposed contrasts, wolves lying down with hares, men creeping into the stomachs of cows, the Empedocles quotation ending in a jumble of up-to-date vulgarisms, and the midwife's prophecy ending in a *lapalissade*.

The monologue of Gargantua in *Pantagruel* 3 has been criti-cized as ridiculing the speaker, chiefly by Brault and Defaux ('Ung Abysme de Science', *BHR*, XXVIII (1966), p.618, and *18*, p.48); but see Lebègue ('Rabelais et la Parodie', *BHR*, XIV (1952), pp.201-03) and Screech (*41*, pp.57-60). It must be remembered that at this point the wise Gargantua of *Gargantua* 50 or even *Pantagruel* 8 has not developed; the Gargantua of the chronicles is simple, docile and affectionate. Rabelais offers a portrait which, although a stylized caricature, is already more rounded and detailed; in 1537 he softens the harsh effect of 'envoye ces pauvres' by making Gargantua add 'baille ce qu'ilz demandent' (*2*, p.233). What Rabelais is ridiculing is the scholastic logic which entangles Gargantua in his 'argumens sophisticques' (*2*, p.232) and the courtly and elegiac clichés, 'la plus cecy, la plus cela, qui feust au monde ... vivre sans elle ne m'est que languir', which get between him and reality.

In the first chapters of *Pantagruel* and, still more, of *Gargantua* Rabelais seems to be deliberately displaying his tech-niques as a comic writer in order to familiarize his audience with them before he moves on to more basically serious matters. These techniques include, as Carol Clarke's book (*15*) recognizes, a consid-erable amount of vulgarity (although this amount should not be over-stated); some is obscene, more is scatological. For a century and a half Rabelais used to be defended by saying that sixteenth-century standards were unlike ours; his standards may be thought to be only too like ours in a time when the printed word is often still more explicit than he is about sex, though perhaps a little less so about excretion. He is explicit; but not for the sake of corrupting. For Rabelais, nature is unfallen (cf. *28*, pp.162-72), or, if fallen, has been redeemed, along with human souls, human language and human bodies; and the resources of all are available to be enjoyed and used to the full. They can be used as material for laughter, to exhibit verbal virtuosity, or as weapons by which assertions are reinforced and enemies insulted. But Rabelais's oaths and imprecations are 'couleurs de rethorique Ciceroniane' (2, p.150), the growl of a nursery lion, terrifying only to the enemies against whom he is the reader's protector.[7]

However, his humour in the early chapters of *Gargantua* depends chiefly on the method of parody which has already shown itself in *Pantagruel* 1 and 3. Parody is not necessarily a destructive technique aiming to produce disbelief. Equally, it can aim sheerly to amuse, by showing how near the comic imitation can come to the serious original; in this way, the mediaeval church allowed a Boy-Bishop or Bishop of Fools to be enthroned for the duration of a particular festival, the real bishop resuming unquestioned authority afterwards. Midway between these two aims, parody may be intended to induce readers or hearers to think clearly, as might, for instance, the mediaeval Gospel of the Silver Mark. Introducing his edition of *Pantagruel* (3, p.xx), Saulnier argues that the book's essential lesson is 'la formation critique d'un jugement simple et droit'. (See also Demerson and Céard in *ER*, XXI; and *45, passim*.)

The beginning of *Gargantua* parodies the beginning of the giant's life in the chronicles, but also that of a saint's or epic hero's life in mediaeval tradition, that of a mythological or historical hero's life as told by classical authors such as Plutarch, and, still more, the ways in which an author might try to win credence for the marvels recounted. *Gargantua* 1 quotes a string of authorities, weighty but irrelevant ones such as Plato and Horace, the relevant but weightless *Pantagruel* itself, and generally accepted but irrelevant ideas such as those of the Wheel of Fortune and the *translatio imperii*, the 'transport des regnes et empires' by which (according to the French) France had providentially been promoted to being the dominant power of the world. It even claims divine inspiration, 'par don

---

[7] For other defences of Rabelais on this count, see *8, passim; 36*, pp.111-19; and, in terms of Lacanian psychology, De Rocher in *ER*, XXI.

souverain des cieulx nous a esté reservée l'antiquité et geneallogie de Gargantua' (2, p.12), inspiration alleged to have come through proceedings which are clearly a parody of contemporary archaeological ones. The poet Maurice Scève, for example, discovered in 1533 in the neighbourhood of Avignon a tomb with

> une grande pierre sans aucune lettre ni autre signe
> inscrit, sauf deux écus d'armes effacés par le temps ...
> une rose figurée au-dessus des écus ...
> des vestiges d'ossements: une mâchoire entière, et
> auprès d'elle une boîte de plomb liée d'un fil de cuivre ...
> une feuille pliée et scellée de cire verte, avec une
> médaille de bronze ...
> un sonnet difficile à lire, parce que les lettres écrites
> sur les plis étaient effacées par le temps.[8]

From the initials M.L.M.I. on the medal Scève rashly deduced that the tomb was that of Petrarch's Laura. Rabelais gives us the remarkably parallel information that Jean Audeau (Jean O d'O, John Nobody of Nowhere?)[9] found outside Chinon

> un grand tombeau de bronze, long sans mesure, car
> oncques n'en trouverent le bout ...
> signé, au dessus, d'un goubelet ...
> neuf flaccons ... desquelz celluy qui au mylieu estoit
> couvroit un gros, gras, grand, gris, joly, petit, moisy
> livret ...
> ladicte geneallogie ... escripte au long de lettres ...
> non en papier, non en parchemin, non en cere, mais en
> escorce d'ulmeau ... usées par vetusté ...
> un petit traicté ... Les rats et blattes, ou ... aultres
> malignes ... bestes, avoient brousté le commencement ...

---

[8] V.-L. Saulnier, *Maurice Scève*, Paris, 1948, I, p.41, translating an Italian text by Jean de Tournes. The paragraphing, like that in the quotation which follows (2, p.13), is ours. See, however, *45*, pp.301-14.

[9] The arabic nought was pronounced O (more fully, 'O en chiffre') at least as early as 1573 (Jean de la Taille, *Les Corrivaus*, I, iv).

With mock-scrupulous 'reverence de l'antiquaille' Rabelais edits in *Gargantua* 2 what purports to be this 'petit traicté', 'Les Fanfreluches antidotées', 'A Galimatia of extravagant conceits', as Rabelais's first and brilliant English translator, Sir Thomas Urquhart, explained it. These verses are not so much a parody as a nonsense-poem of a type then much in vogue, the *(épître du) coq à l'âne*,[10] a string of phrases which, though each is grammatically correct in itself, add up to absurdity. Topical allusions glimmer through the 'Fanfreluches' (and, if *11*, II, pp.29-89, is right, sexual allusions too), with perhaps a vague chain of thought: at the beginning, some person with religious affiliations (the Pope?) makes a strong initial impression but finds his pretensions exposed and retires into private life; at the end, a good and prosperous king (Grandgousier or Gargantua?) will be succeeded by a still greater (Gargantua or Pantagruel?) who will overthrow his enemy (Picrochole or Anarche?) and establish a Utopia — or a Thélème? (On Rabelais's use of contemporary verse forms, sometimes deliberately archaizing, see Mireille Huchon in *RIB*.)

Gargantua 3 asserts the possibility and legitimacy of the giant's birth after an eleven-month pregnancy. The possibility of such a pregnancy was at the time being warmly discussed, by doctors and therefore also by lawyers. Rabelais hints at their arguments through a series of allusions, more or less relevant, firstly to parallel wonders in classical mythology, then to medical and legal authorities, poets and even the comic playwright Plautus, and finally to the consequences of the possibility for merry or unscrupulous widows. According to Screech (*41*, pp.132-34), he is attacking the 'tolerant traditionalist school' of lawyers, as he certainly does elsewhere; according to Antonioli (*6*, pp.161-64), he is glorifying human instincts.

To give a new kind of pseudo-support to the author's assertions, the next three chapters invoke realistic detail. Like all farmers of the age, Grandgousier appears to have slaughtered a large number

---

[10] See C.A. Mayer, 'Coq-à-l'âne. Definition - Invention - Attributions', *French Studies*, XVI (1962), pp.1-13; and his edition, *Clément Marot: Œuvres satiriques*, London, 1962, pp.8-14.

of his beasts just before Lent, to provide salt meat for the weeks after Easter and incidentally an enormous feast on Shrove Tuesday. *Gargantua* 4 explains these very reasonable proceedings with the help of dialectal technical terms, each of which turns out to be so esoteric that it has to be defined for the reader with the help of another. Rabelais's real knowledge of local dialect is thus so clearly established that we are invited by implication to assume his equal knowledgeability about the date, local topography, and the physiological consequences of the pregnant Gargamelle's over-eating. *Gargantua* 5 could almost be taken for a transcript of a tape-recording of the increasingly tipsy talk of the guests at Grandgousier's feast. Rabelais has seen to it that from their remarks the sex, profession or tone of individual speakers can often be deduced, so as to confirm the impression we receive that he was there himself and knew them personally. (On both chapters 4 and 5 see especially *16*, pp.3-15; on 5 see also *11*, II, pp.110-83.)

The pseudo-appeal of *Gargantua* 6, beyond authority and experience, is to faith. Here it is particularly important to compare the first edition with that of 1542. In both, a Latin syntax ennobles the scene, with an opening construction modelled on the classical ablative absolute, 'Eulx tenens', with subordinating conjunctions, 'dont ... encores que ... en sorte que ...', and with reported speech; yet, in both, such Latinism clashes laughably with a colloquial vocabulary that down-grades the characters, 'se porter mal du bas', 'poupon', and the untranslateable joke by which Grandgousier likens his wife to a mare. This rich counterpoint modulates into a Biblical allusion, 'la joye qui toust succederoit luy tolliroit tout cest ennuy, en sorte que seulement ne luy en resteroit la soubvenance.'

Grandgousier proceeds, in all the earlier editions, to quote the exact words of John XVI, 21, in French, a use of the New Testament which his wife ranks above the superstitious use of a Catholic saint's life to relieve the pain of childbirth, 'mieulx m'en trouve que de ouyr la vie de saincte Marguerite ou quelque aultre capharderie.' Whether Rabelais is here expressing a genuine Evangelicalism on the giants' part or on his own, or merely using Evangelical expressions to hit at unenlightened Catholic superstition, he felt it safer in 1542 to delete

both speeches and substitute a second crude masculine joke by
Grandgousier and a feminist retort by Gargamelle. These fill the gap
and permit the transition back to her yet cruder, equally jocular
mock-prayer in all editions: 'Mais pleust à Dieu que vous l'eussiez
coupé'.

Gargamelle's prolapse could well be the result of indigestion,
in fiction as it could have been in life. The medical treatment applied
is not abnormal; rather more so are its results, culminating in the
birth of Gargantua through her ear. But, says the narrator in all
editions, 'un homme de bien, un homme de bon sens, croit tousjours
ce qu'on luy dict et qu'il trouve par escript' (2, p.31). This is
supported in every edition, including that of 1542, by the naïve
commonplaces by which a literal-minded Catholic (or Evangelical?)
might support the accounts of Biblical miracles: Scripture does not
say it was not so — it could have been so had it been God's will —
to God nothing is impossible. Before 1542, it had been supported
also by more exact Biblical quotations more mischievously used:
'innocens credit omni verbo' (Proverbs XIV, 15), which means not,
as might be thought, that an innocent man believes all he hears, but
that a fool does; 'charitas omnia credit' (I Corinthians XIII, 7), which
means not that love believes everything, but that it believes the best
of anyone; and 'foy est argument des choses de nulle apparence'
(Hebrews XI, 1), which means 'faith is the means through which we
believe what lies beyond the scope of the senses', but which Rabelais
invites us to mistranslate, 'faith is an argument about things with no
likelihood'.

Is all this, as Screech says (*41*, pp.134-37), 'evangelical propa-
ganda at its best', or, as Busson says (*13*, pp.165-67), rationalist
hitting at both Catholicism and Evangelicalism? Rabelais, for the
moment, leaves us guessing, and escapes into a series, growing with
successive editions, of mythological parallels and perhaps inventions
of his own about folklore characters, 'Rocquetaillade nasquit il pas
du talon de sa mere?' (2, p.32). Ambiguity continues, for both
Catholics and Evangelicals might protest at the placing of such
fictions on a level with Biblical truths; but Rabelais could retort that
he is merely placing pagan fiction on a level with his own.

He offers a final pseudo-proof of his reliability as an authority, as he did in *Pantagruel* 1, in the shape of his own capacity for quasi-scholarly scepticism. Even this device is to be found in germ in *Les Grandes et Inestimables Cronicques*: 'Aulcuns acteurs veullent dire que Gargantua fut totallement nourry de chairs en son enfance. Je dis que non (ainsi que dit Morgain et plusieurs aultres)'; but as usual Rabelais goes further, parodying both humanistic and scholastic pedantry. The famous first-century scientific compendium, Pliny's *Historia Naturalis*, is far more incredible, concludes *Gargantua* 6, than Rabelais's own story. The notion that Gargantua's mother breast-fed him, asserts *Gargantua* 7, 'n'est vraysemblable'; it is indeed, says the narrator, an example of the heterodoxy of the Scotists, and has been declared (before 1542, he says 'par Sorbone') 'scandaleuse, des pitoyables aureilles offensive, et sentent de loing heresie' (2, pp.33-34). How, Rabelais would ask tongue-in-cheek, can he himself be accused of heresy, or of lacking the sense of what is 'vraysemblable', when his own judgment in such matters can be seen to be so delicate and precise?

3. The Hero's Childhood: Pantagruel 4 and Gargantua 7-13

The mental and moral evolution of the hero through successive stages will be one of Rabelais's themes, perhaps his main theme, throughout his two books; but of course the hero's education must be prepared for by a picture of his childhood, prodigious in itself but capable of development. Details emphasizing the strength and prowess of the hero even in his infancy are to be found in almost every giant-story; but at this point the jokes of *Les Grandes et Inestimables Cronicques* turn solely on the child Gargantua's size. He throws at the birds stones twice as big as millstones, goads his parents' mare with a stick the length of a mast, wounds his own toe with a two-hundred-pound thorn, and splints it with a church-steeple tied on with a four-hundred-ell bandage 'sauf demy quartier justement'; in this the *Cronicques* use the comic precision which we have already seen Rabelais inheriting, and which he will elsewhere increase.

Pantagruel 4 considerably enriches this material with the help of contributions from a variety of sources. Some details are transferred from other parts of the *Cronicques*: the size of the giant's meal (*Cronicques*, sig. B iiii v⁰, a four-course dinner with two hundred oxen as the main dish); the business of making a saucepan for him (*Cronicques*, sig. B iii v⁰, a club). Occasionally the *Cronicques* use local references to supply verisimilitude, as when Grandgousier lays down a rock he has been carrying, which becomes the Mont St Michel (sig. B ii); *Pantagruel* 4 takes this device much further, with references to towns famous for ironmongery (Saumur and Villedieu), for archaeological remains (Bourges), for rope-making (Tain) and for harbours (Le Havre, La Rochelle). Rabelais mentions literary analogues, Biblical (Samson and Lucifer) and classical

(Hercules, by the account of Pindar), and also direct sources (Pliny and Nicolas de Lyra, rather more of a sceptic than Rabelais suggests). The short space of *Pantagruel* 4 packs all these effects together with unprecedented concision. It adds a wealth of vivid images (the wolves, cormorant, chicken, tortoise and galleon) and of imaginative exaggeration (Pantagruel's eating the cow and bear, and carrying and smashing his cradle), and suggests not merely Pantagruel's size (never stated precisely or implied consistently, any more than Gargantua's) but also his strength, enterprise, gusto and ingenuity.

These qualities also appear in Rabelais's much more detailed portrait of the child Gargantua; but the emphasis is shifted. *Gargantua* 7-13 presents (*pace 6*, pp.176-80) a far happier child than the sometimes frustrated and ferocious Pantagruel. His birth-cry, 'A boyre!' (2, p.33), shows the enjoyment of food and drink which characterized chapters 4-5; he travels in his go-cart 'joyeusement ... et ne crioit que bien peu' (2, p.34); drink immediately stops his crying, and the very tinkle of glasses sends him into 'ecstase' (ib.); and his relationship with his nurses (ch. 11, 2, pp.49-50), however premature the sexuality involved, is undoubtedly a friendly and happy one. His father Grandgousier, at first pictured only as a comfortable peasant farmer, turns out to be a king, marrried to a princess (ch. 3, 2, p.19), conqueror of the Canary Islands (ch. 13, 2, p.54), and possessed of unlimited resources. Gargantua is evidently to be a giant not merely in size but in all his attributes and attainments, with neither natural barriers nor unnatural restrictions to hinder his full development in all ways.

All sides of life, Rabelais appears to be saying, are to be enjoyed: the beautiful but also the ugly (hence ch. 13); the curious and rare but also the ordinary; the magnificent costume supplied to Gargantua, but also the simple pleasures of the peasants. Rabelais really likes both these pleasures and these peasants; the fun he makes of them is friendly. The people of whom he makes unfriendly fun are those who reject some aspect of life, pedants and bigots, prudes and philistines, and hostile critics of his own books (see the last pages of the Prologues and of *Pantagruel*).

All stages of life are to be enjoyed; and first, childhood. Rabelais's message is shown even in the elaborate costume designed for Gargantua in chapter 8, which bores some critics (e.g. Berlioz, *11*, II, pp.213-14), but which can be fascinating if studied with the help of a full-length contemporary portrait such as those of François I or Henry VIII. *Les Grandes et Inestimables Cronicques* designed a livery for the adult Gargantua, but stressed only its size, its combination of yellow and red, and Gargantua's expensive signet-ring. Rabelais's two-year-old wears an adult costume as four- or five-year-olds did in fact then, but one which makes the most of the enjoyable possibilities of dress. It is rich and fashionable, as is shown by the jewellery, silver and gold embroidery, and *deschicqueture* or 'slashing' of ornamental slits into costly material to reveal an equally costly lining; but the yellow and red of the *Cronicques* are replaced more tastefully by white and blue. Some details are suggested by sheer jocularity; thus the single undergar-ment, the *chemise* or shirt, is made with *coussons* (gussets) rather than *fronsure* (gathers), which permits a sexy joke. Over it is worn the *pourpoinct* or doublet, the close-fitting tunic, sometimes skirted, to which the *chausses* (hose or breeches) are fastened by means of *agueillettes* (tags or laces). Over this come the *saye*, a loose-fitting jacket, and the *ceinture*, additionally useful in that weapons and (in days before pockets) wallets could hang from it. Over all comes the *robbe* or gown, the academic forms of which are still worn.

Some of the accessories are excitingly exotic, such as the rings, the pearls from the Persian Gulf, the pelican's feather in the hat, and the goblin-skin gloves trimmed with werewolf-fur; but the *chausses*, *braguette* and hat are of a healthy capacity, and the weapons are of local make and peaceable. The importance of sex in the full life is emphasized by the *braguette*, heavily adorned, particularly with two emeralds which have on Gargantua just the opposite effect from that traditionally attributed to them, the preser-vation of chastity. The importance of sexual love, close friendship, or both is emphasized by the hat-brooch, featuring Plato's Androgyne (*Symposium*, 189-93), but with significant alterations. Plato's imagined primitive human being had 'one head to two faces, which looked opposite ways';[11] Rabelais provides a second head so that the two faces can look at each other; and his Greek motto comes not from Plato but from the New Testament, in the Authorized Version 'Charity seeketh not her own' (I Corinthians XIII, 5), but taken by Rabelais to imply 'He who loves seeks his other half'.

Chapter 8 includes, at intervals, hits at pedants who argue about what is the colour of a pigeon's neck, and whether hose should be laced to the doublet or vice versa. This approach dominates chapters 9 and 10, where Rabelais's substitution of blue and white for the yellow and red of the *Cronicques* receives a mock-justification based on parody of contemporary techniques of controversy at their worst (see *31*, pp.209-15, and *41*, pp.137-43). Theories of the symbolism of colours (as also of gems and other natural objects) were then much in vogue, highly esteemed but widely varying. Rabelais singles out for attack a real work, the *Blason des couleurs* of Sicile and Carroset, which chapter 9 attacks with a battery of invective: opprobrious epithets and slangy parentheses; an appeal to reason against mere authority, 'l'usance des tyrans' (2, p.40); a satire of arbitrary heraldic devices and punning mottoes; and an expressed preference for devices based on true classical scholarship, 'par auctoritez receues et approuvées de toute ancienneté' (2, pp.42-43).

On such a basis, with help from nearly thirty sources ranging from Aristotle and Plutarch to the Bible and Erasmus, chapter 10 constructs a half-comic, half-serious argument that white symbolizes joy, concluding with impudent perfunctoriness that 'similarly, blue symbolizes heaven'. The whole matter has not been worth discussing, as Rabelais knows perfectly well and implies when he points out that anyone could have discussed it: 'Par mesmes raisons (si raisons les doibz nommer et non resveries) ferois je paindre un *penier*, denotant qu'on me faict *pener*' (2, p.42). The function of the two chapters is to show off his versatile ingenuity, and, subtly, to help towards swinging the reader's allegiance from late mediaeval authorities to genuine classical ones.

---

[11] *Symposium*, 189E, tr. W.R.M. Lamb, London (Heinemann), 1946. See *41*, pp.142-43, but also J. Schwarz in *ER*, XIV (1977), pp.265 ff.

The theme of the happiness of Gargantua's childhood is renewed in chapter 11 (see *31*, pp.508-14), a mere 330-word idyll in its first version, but doubled in length by 1542. Where real-life custom discounted children until they could dress as adults and mix with adults (see *7*, p.134), and edifying fiction showed the child-prodigy as a paragon of virtue or heroism, Rabelais spends longer than most authors before his time, or in it, painting childhood for its own sake. There is no mention here of gigantic size or unnatural precocity of any sort except the sexual. The four-year-old Gargantua has complete freedom to enjoy the natural, the trivial and, in the 1542 edition, the impossible; the additions of that date are mostly based on traditional proverbs advising against the inappropriate, the useless and the impracticable. Gargantua cheerfully ignores all the prohibitions: 'se asseoyt entre deux selles le cul à terre, se couvroyt d'un sac mouillé ... gardoyt la lune des loups ...'; and he benefits from the positive advice: 'congnoissoyt mousches en laict ... vouloyt que maille à maille on feist les haubergeons ... faisoyt de necessité vertus ...'

Spoiling by his governesses does him no harm; to the age of five his progress is good. His childhood exploits do not include the military ones of an epic hero, nor even the physical ones of Pantagruel; Rabelais has his reasons for putting these much later; but they do include intellectual ones. Chapter 12, whose point is missed by many critics (even *10*, p.73; *15*, p.10; *16*, p.177; and *26*, pp.86-87; but see G. Spillebout in *BARD*, III, 6 (1977), pp.246-49) shows a Gargantua intelligent enough to keep from potential enemies the secret of the stables of his father's war-horses ('grands chevaux'). The names of the visitors Painensac and Francrepas are highly suspicious, and the steward and harbinger behave as spies, 'demandans secrettement où estoient les estables des grands chevaulx, pensans que voluntiers les enfans decellent tout' (2, p.51). Gargantua deliberately fools the outsiders, leading them from room to room, by staircase after staircase to his own nursery; caps their discomfiture with taunts and cross-talk (on *avoir le moine* see *11*, II, pp.330-34, and on *aubeliere* P. Burrell in *ER*, XI (1974), p.146, and K. Baldinger in *ER*, XIII (1976), p.181); and sends them away predicting that one day he will do great things, 'je te voirray quelque jour pape'.

On the basis of Gargantua's experiments in chapter 13 (see *15*, pp.97-99 and 170-71, and Rigolot in *ER*, XXI and in *RIB*) his father comes to a similar conclusion: Gargantua deserves, not merely the usual education of a young noble in fighting, hunting and the social graces, but an academic education which will lead him (2, p.60) 'à degré souverain de sapience'. We shall see what results.

4. The Hero's Education, and Rabelais's Sincerity: Pantagruel 5-8 and Gargantua 14-24

Les Grandes et Inestimables Cronicques contain no account of the hero's education; he visits Paris after his parents' death, but only because 'il appetoit a veoir choses nouvelles comme font jeunes gens'. The education of Rabelais's Pantagruel takes place bit by bit, less at a single university than through his reactions to his tour of several, in chapter 5, and less through those reactions than through his encounters with different opponents in later chapters. Chapter 8 offers what appears to be a systematic study of education; it is not a direct account of the hero's experience so much as the text of a letter to him from his father Gargantua. By the time Rabelais wrote this chapter he was evidently thinking deeply about education, but not yet ready to incorporate his thoughts explicitly into the story-line of *Pantagruel*. These thoughts had been systematized by the time he wrote *Gargantua*, which devotes to them eleven chapters. In both books the giants' size fades into the background; they can read books of normal format and play squash with human companions (2, pp.89 and 243); though their stamina, at least, remains prodigious.

Pantagruel's 'escole' at Poitiers (2, p.239) would have been an institution attached to the university, and, in the French fashion of the time (see 7, p.150), prepared to take beginners of seven or eight as well as arts students proceeding to their B.A. or M.A., although the latter were free to move on at will to other universities. Chapter 5's tour of the universities of France was formerly used as evidence that Rabelais made a similar one; he would certainly have made acquaintance first with Poitiers, but allusions such as those to Bordeaux, Toulouse and Avignon could be based on the briefest of excursions or mere hearsay. However, Rabelais does characterize the Montpellier and Bourges of his day with some justice, while sugaring his pills with jokes about local antiquities and activities. (On the execution of Jean de Caturce at Toulouse, 2, p.241, see *41*, pp.72-73). What is more, he hints at principles important to him: the profitable use of time, a modern approach to law, a modern and cheerful approach to medicine, and religious tolerance.

The meeting with the Limousin scholar in chapter 6 (see especially *30*, pp.73-79, and J. Parkin in *ER*, XVIII (1985), pp.60-62) contains puzzles: why should Pantagruel raise such strong objections to a use of Latin derivatives which may seem not very different from that of Rabelais himself, or from Panurge's use of pure Latin in chapter 9? The Limousin's speeches are comprehensible to anyone who has studied Latin, as Pantagruel must have by this stage; they stem from an old joke, quoted by Geofroy Tory in 1529:

> Quant Escumeurs de Latin disent, Despumon la verbocination latiale, et transfreton la Sequane au dilucule et crepuscule, puis deambulon par les Quadrivies et Platees de Lutece, et comme verisimiles amorabundes captivon la benivolence de lomnigene et omniforme sexe feminin, me semble quilz ne se moucquent seullement de leurs semblables, mais de leur mesme Personne. (*Champ Fleury*, ed. G. Cohen, Paris, 1931, sig. A viii)

This parody of Latinization evidently did not originate with Tory, and it is not known how far Rabelais was quoting and at what point he started making his own additions. Does Pantagruel really not understand the language being parodied? Gray (*26*, p.45) argues that at this stage he does not understand anyone. Or does he pretend not to understand? Is it a matter of a clash of personalities rather than of linguistic theories? The Limousin is plainly a silly and affected coward, whose interests are less in study than in sex and drink, and whose piety shows signs of both superficiality and bigotry. However, the criticisms voiced by Pantagruel's companion, 'ce gallant veult contrefaire la langue des Parisians; mais il ne faict que escorcher le latin ...', and repeated by Pantagruel himself (2, pp.246-47), are purely linguistic ones: the Limousin's language is neither genuine Latin nor genuine French, only an attempt to be fashionably unusual. Pantagruel forces him to speak 'naturellement', a term which might call for much comment; but the narrator himself explains it: 'il nous convient parler selon le langage usité, et ... eviter les motz espaves' ('absurdes' in editions before 1534). Presumably (cf. R. Lebègue, *Revue des cours et conférences*, 2ᵉ série, XL (1939), pp.303-14), Rabelais is saying, 'Have some common sense; words are fun, but don't go too far!'

In chapter 7 the University of Paris is characterized on the lines used in chapter 5; but the satire here (more than trebled in length between the first edition and 1542) is especially aimed at the library of the Abbey of Saint-Victor, famous in its time, but made by Rabelais into a symbol of all he hates in out-of-date culture.[12] A few of the book-titles, and rather more of the authors' names, are genuine; thus the first title, *Bigua salutis*, is an authentic example of those often given in the period to works of edification, like the English *Castle of Perseverance* or *Mirror for Magistrates*. However, Berlioz (*11*, I, p.55) and De Grève (*ER*, XXI) can see an obscene pun even in that first title, still more in those which parody it. Soon come hints at the gluttony, lustfulness and bigotry of clerics and nuns and the venality of lawyers, and attacks on the authority of the Vatican and (after the first edition) the sale of indulgences. Above all come hits at the conservatism, pedantry and dirtiness of the 'Sorbonici' (*2*, p.254), their reliance on second-hand learning and their claims to impossible knowledge ('*De Cosmographia Purgatorii*', '*De Castrametandis Crinibus*'). The exclusively theological Collège de la Sorbonne was the usual meeting-place of the Paris Faculty of Theology, which could advise the *Parlement* on censoring any French publication touching on religion. This made the Faculty and the college special objects of Rabelais's attacks, though in 1542 many in this chapter and elsewhere are deleted or veiled, more or less.

---

[12] See *23*, pp.316-21; A.H. Schutz, *Modern Language Notes*, LXX (1955), pp.39-41; and *41*, pp.44, 60-63 and 113-16.

Pantagruel's education appears to reach a climax in chapter 8, a great enigma for critics. (Among general studies, G. Seiver's 'Cicero's *De Oratore* and Rabelais', *PMLA*, LIX (1944), pp.655-71, is richer than the title might suggest.) Gargantua's letter seems to provide valuable evidence of how the Renaissance was seen by one who lived during it. But suspicions have been aroused by the over-stating of the case: the past is painted as jet-black, 'encores tenebreux et sentant l'infelicité et la calamité des Gothz' (*2*, p.258), the present as snow-white, 'tout le monde est plein de gens savans'; and a gigantic curriculum is advocated, 'que je voy[e] un abysme de science' (*2*, p.261). The idea that, unless Pantagruel were to prove a worthy successor to his father, Gargantua would 'totallement mourir' (*2*, p.257) was seen by Lefranc as subtly suggesting that Rabelais disbelieved in eternal life in the Christian sense (*1*, III, pp.xliii-xlv); Febvre answered with emphasis on the sixteenth-century under-standing of death as the separation of body and soul (*23*, pp.183-225, though see E.V. Telle, *BHR*, XIX (1957), pp.208-33): only if Pantagruel takes after his father in both respects will the images of Gargantua's body and soul survive united in this world. But even apart from this phrase, the style of the letter, with its weighty polysyllables and profound abstractions, seems inconsistent with the rest of *Pantagruel*.

Using the fact that the first edition follows this chapter with two numbered '9', C.A. Béné (*Paedagogica Historica*, I (1961), pp.39 ff.) put forward an interesting theory (which convinced Screech, *BHR*, XXV (1963), pp.480-82) that the letter was added at the last minute; Rabelais or his printer would then have renumbered the original 'chapter 8' to make it 9, but forgotten to renumber the chapters thereafter. Brault saw the whole letter as a hoax (*12*), 'a friendly parody of humanistic concerns'; for him, 'Rabelais derides the notion that anyone could possibly acquire *tout sçavoir* and *toutes sciences*'. For Rigolot (*36*, pp.55-62) the letter is a study in one register of expression, 'un sujet emprunté qui nous est livré dans une langue empruntée'. For Defaux (*18*, pp.xi-xii) it is simultaneously serious and comic. For Gray (*26*, pp.43 and 90-91) it is serious, but comic in its context, since Pantagruel does not profit from it. La

Charité (*L'Esprit Créateur*, XXI (1981), pp.26-39) replies that were it parody, Rabelais would have indicated that it should be read as such; it is rather 'intertextual gamesmanship'.

But how can we be sure what interpretation is nearest to the truth? or be sure whether the similar curriculum of *Gargantua* 23-24 is serious or is also a hoax? Defaux (*ER*, XI (1974), p.134) goes on to suggest this: Gargantua passes 'de l'extrême paresse à l'extrême surmenage'. Before him, Beaujour and Rigolot had suggested the same: 'L'éducation de Gargantua n'est pas moins comique sous Ponocrates que sous ses précepteurs théologiens' (*10*, p.28), 'En prenant la partie opposée à la fainéantise, Rabelais sait qu'il dresse un tableau tout aussi grotesque ... Rabelais s'amuse' (*36*, p.71); and Berlioz sees the young Eudemon of chapter 15 as a caricature (*11*, II, p.415). How are we to know when Rabelais is being serious, if ever?

La Charité asserts (art. cit., pp.28-29) that 'countless other elements would have to buttress and enhance the parodic possibility ... At no point is there any kind of tonal contrast or disjunction between what is articulated and how it is articulated.' Dorothy Coleman contends that 'the distinctive stylistic character of the letter confirms its serious intent' (*16*, p.186). Demerson declares that 'le discours sérieux se reconnaît à ce qu'il remet en place une idée qui avait été déformée par la mauvaise rhétorique ...' (*20*, p.14; and cf. *21*, p.81). But one might reply that the tone of the narrator in the undoubtedly parodic *Gargantua* 10, and of Thaumaste in *Pantagruel* 18 and 20, is just as unified and, at first glance, serious; and one could argue, tongue-in-cheek, that these chapters too are reinstating ideas previously obscured.

Screech (*41*, pp.409-32) offers a more complicated argument to the effect that Rabelais answers our question in his *Quart Livre*, and especially in its chapters 55 and 56. 'Actions speak louder' than words (p.409); if a Rabelaisian giant laughs at his opponents, or shows 'gracious magnanimity' to them, we may conclude that the author is behind him. Words convey truth if, and only if, 'the arbitrary imposition of the word-creator' correlates with 'the acceptance of the symbol by convention' (p.416); *Pantagruel* 8 and *Gargantua* 23-24 use conventional, though elevated, expression, as the Limousin scholar does not. Finally, says Screech, one can distinguish truth from error and perversity by its correlation with 'truth supernaturally revealed' (p.431). But one might reply to Screech that if Rabelais hid the key to his thought in chapters only to be published in 1552, he kept his readers waiting for an inordinate time, and not without risk to himself.

A work cannot authenticate itself or prove its own seriousness, as La Charité, Dorothy Coleman, Demerson and even Screech want it to do. However serious the giants may claim to be, however much the narrator may insist that serious they are, a reader can still comment, 'What perfect parody!' Nor can the subjective reactions of other readers testify to the seriousness of a work; it is no solution to say 'It rings true' — a good parodist will see to it that it does. Can even outside evidence prove a work to be serious when the author is not concerned to make that seriousness clear, or is concerned not to make it clear? And if not, what can?

Perhaps, one may venture to suggest, the convergence of strong internal and external evidence, in the same way in which evidence given in a law-court can be supported by evidence of character. Rabelais was not so much a monk by upbringing and a theologian by training, as a doctor by a vocation which overrode any former monastic one. As a practising doctor, he seems to have relied on observation, common sense and a good 'bedside manner'; evidence of the first and second qualities is provided by his share in a dissection in 1530 (see *6*, p.61), and of the second and third, perhaps of all three, by his being selected as personal medical attendant by the experienced, urbane and practical brothers Bishop Jean du Bellay (later Cardinal) and Guillaume de Langey. Perhaps one may assume at least that Rabelais is basically serious, that he is reflecting, however comically, his own sincere and positive views, when his characters similarly resort to observation and react with common sense — with a just indignation, with a sense of humour, or with the prudence which Gargantua will show in chapters 50 and 51. If, contrariwise, what inspired Rabelais was a vein of scepticism denying the value of all knowledge, one would be left wondering why his patrons did not choose a more reliable medical adviser.

A doctor who insinuates, however discreetly, either that 'science is bunk' or that communication is impossible will not win the confidence of his patients.

Assuming that the constructive parts of *Pantagruel* 8, *Gargantua* 15 and *Gargantua* 23-24 are fundamentally serious, despite their inclusion of sporadic 'cues for laughter' (*16*, p.178) and especially of Rabelais's characteristic exaggeration, let us look in rather more detail at the treatment of education in *Gargantua*.

All but one of the chapters from 14 to 22 inclusive are illustrations of 'how not to do it'. The grotesque course of education on which Grandgousier launches his son in chapter 14 is founded on a certain stratum of fact, though caricatured and, by Rabelais's own time, out of date. Under a first tutor with a fine Old Testament name, Gargantua studies at snail's pace the alphabet ('sa charte'), the basics of Latin grammar ('*Donat*'), and specimens of the other two parts of the mediaeval *trivium* or Threefold Way, rhetoric and logic, in the shape of two fairly simple readers on good behaviour ('le *Facet*' and Alanus) and one ('*Theodolet*') on the contrast of truth with falsehood. Extending his grammatical studies to the *modi significandi*, the Forms of Expression, with the help of many imaginary commentaries by absurdly-named authors but no original works, Gargantua becomes able, after over thirty-seven years in all, to prove 'sus ses doigts' that 'there is no science of the Forms of Expression'.

Before he can complete his next study, the Church calendar ('le *Compost*'), his tutor dies of venereal disease. To make sure, a successor, again absurdly named, takes the pupil back to the beginning of his course: more elementary Latin grammar (Hugutius, Everard de Béthune, etc.), more etiquette for children (*De moribus in mensa servandis*), and ready-made sermons (*Dormi secure*). It is not surprising that Gargantua becomes as 'saige' (*2*, p.62), not as anyone *fourni*, turned out later, but as anyone *fourné*, put into a baking-oven.

His journey to Paris, in chapters 16 and 17, develops the very few borrowings made at this point from *Les Grandes et Inestimables Cronicques*: the antics of the gigantic mare (a present from Merlin in the *Cronicques*, from an Algerian king in *Gargantua*) and the pranks of Gargantua himself while resting on the roof of Notre Dame.

Rabelais seems concerned to portray Gargantua's psychology at this stage with some complexity; he is a lout, stunted by his bad education, but not really malicious, and not without a certain rough wit and charm, which the adaptations of the *Cronicques* are well calculated to convey: 'considera les grosses cloches ... et les feist sonner bien harmonieusement. Ce que faisant, luy vint en pensée qu'elles serviroient bien de campanes au coul de sa jument' (ch. 17, 2, p.69, where 'bien harmonieusement' and 'serviroient bien' have no equivalent in the *Cronicques*). Relevant to education is Grandgousier's spoonerism (2, p.66), which ought to read, 'Si n'estoient messieurs les clercs, nous vivrions comme bestes', 'if it were not for learned men, we should all be barbarians', but which Grandgousier contorts to suggest, 'if it were not for stupid academics, we should all live in comfort'.

The stupid academics, the end-products of the education caricatured, do not appear in the *Cronicques*, but are seen in action in chapters 17-20. Gargantua, the bright child stunted into a loutish youth, is saved from becoming a stupid old man, but these dodderers show what he might have become. They discuss the disappearance of the Notre-Dame bells in the correct form of a mediaeval disputation, using the logical syllogism, Baralipton, whereby a particular conclusion is deduced from two generalizations, perhaps 'negotiators need wisdom' and 'old men are wise'. Elected negotiator for this reason, Janotus (on whom see especially *16*, pp.106-08 and *11*, II, pp.464-522) shows his 'wisdom' in a splendid drunken garbling of his laboriously prepared rhetorical speech.

It is complete with the remains of an introductory salutation ('*Mna dies* ...'), a statement of the situation ('Ce ne seroyt que bon que nous rendissiez nos cloches ...'), arguments intended to be persuasive ('Si vous nous les rendez ...:'), ill-chosen quotations ('*Reddite* ...'), rebuttal of opposing arguments ('Si vostre jument s'en trouve bien ...'), pseudo-logical proofs ('*Omnis clocha* ...'), emotional appeals ('*in nomine Patris* ...'), a concession to the opposition ('Un quidam latinisateur ...'), and all possible alternatives in the way of transitions ('*Verum enim vero* ...') and concluding formulae ('Et plus n'en dict ...'). Meanwhile he unconsciously betrays his real motives, concern for drink ('si nous perdons le piot, nous perdons tout'), for food and his own comfort ('six pans de saucisses et une bonne paire de chausses'), and for the stamping out of heresy: 'il feut declairé hereticque; nous les faisons comme de cire' (2, p.75).

The same misuse of learning in one's own interests appears in chapter 20, both in Janotus's snubbing of Bandouille ('baudet, tu ne concluds poinct *in modo et figura*', 2, p.77) and in the Sorbonne's refusing Janotus an honorarium after his rewarding by Gargantua. They appeal to 'raison', to which he retorts, 'Nous n'en usons poinct ceans' (2, p.78). The resulting court-case is still continuing, says Rabelais with a fine leap from past to present; and its continuance, he points out, is contrary to the very constitution of the University of Paris, which states that 'Dieu seul peult faire choses infinies' (2, p.79) — although it does all prove the truth of a classical saying, 'le dict de Chilon ...', which would, he implies, be Greek to the Sorbonne.

Against these pictures, and the final picture in chapters 21-22 which surveys all Gargantua's idleness, dirtiness, greed, ignorance, silliness and frivolity at this stage, Rabelais sets in chapter 15 the picture of Eudemon, 'the boy favoured by Fortune', introduced to Grandgousier by a nobleman whose name, Des Marays, may be an approximate anagram of that of D. Erasmus (G. J. Brault, *Kentucky Romance Quarterly*, XVIII (1971), pp.307-17). Eudemon is merely 'quelc'un de ces jeunes gens du temps present, qui ...[a]... seulement estudié deux ans', and is therefore presumably about eight years old; but he has evidently profited from the education described by B.L. Joseph:

> In their teaching ... humanists were inspired by clearly
> formulated convictions respecting the nature of man and
> his place in the universe. They adhered to the normal
> Christian view of man as unique among the inhabitants
> of the earth in virtue of his ... reason ... It showed itself
> in erect stature, grace of movement, beauty of body and
> — most important of all from the point of view of
> education — in speech ... Humanist methods took

advantage of the intimate connexion between reason and
speech to establish training in thought and expression
firmly and prominently in the curriculum ... (*Elizabethan
Acting*, Oxford (1951), ch. 2)

With less than a day's notice, Eudemon is summoned to Grandgousier's court to make an almost impromptu Latin speech, although
he is allowed to choose his own theme. He elects to make a eulogy
of Gargantua, according to the classical rules of rhetoric, so far as he
can apply them to such an unpromising object. Appropriate gestures,
intonation and figures of speech ('languaige ... aorné', 2, p.64)
enhance four sections of descending importance, followed by a
moral conclusion ('reverer son pere') and a postscript in which the
orator seizes the opportunity of asking for a job — and he gets it. He
and his own tutor, Ponocrates, 'the man with power over fatigue',
accompany Gargantua to Paris, for the giant to be re-educated on the
new lines.

These are expounded fully in chapters 23-24, which need little
commentary. Plattard (*1*, I, pp.lxxxviii-xcix), Larmat (*31*), Antonioli
(*6*) and others have traced the sources of Ponocrates's educational
principles and methods; Lote (*33*), Jourda (*28*) and the aforenamed
pick out their chief essentials; Plattard, Lote and later critics indicate
points where they fall short. One may add that at least the first third
of Montaigne's 1580 essay 'De l'institution des enfans' (I, 26) may be
read as a continuous criticism of *Gargantua* 23-24.

Montaigne opens by disclaiming omniscience (perhaps
Gargantua's 'abysme de science', 2, p.261) and attacking quotation-
collecting (perhaps Gargantua's 'passaiges ... competens', 2, p.90).
He goes on to warn against prematurely predicting a child's abilities
('la montre de leurs inclinations'), against delivering lectures to be
merely memorized ('comme qui verseroit dans un entonnoir'),
against relying on mere authority ('par simple authorité et à credit'),
against talking and disputing for their own sake ('emploiter nostre
marchandise'), and even, after 1588, against seeking 'vigueur de
nerfs' rather than 'de coeur' (*Les Essais*, ed. P. Villey and V.-L.
Saulnier, Paris (1965), pp.149, 150, 151, 154, 153). However,

Montaigne was certainly not thinking only of Rabelais, and there is positive praise in his classing the latter's work 'entre les livres simplement plaisans' and 'dignes qu'on s'y amuse' (*qu'on s'en occupe*; 'Des Livres', II, 10, ib., p.410).

Those who criticize Ponocrates's curriculum adversely often overlook several major elements in it. A very important one is the 'cas practicques et concernens l'estat humain, lesquelz ilz estendoient aulcunes foys jusques deux ou troys heures' (2, p.89). These must be understood as comprising practical and topical social studies arising out of what Gargantua had learnt, during which he would surely be trained for kingship by stimulation of his imagination and judgment. Such a training would also be helped by chapter 24's excursions to observe the 'industrie et invention des mestiers' and even the 'ruses' of the 'trejectaires et theriacleurs' (2, p.98).

Also to be noted is an Evangelical colouring, too discreet to be challenged then as heretical or now as parodic, but perceptible to those alert to the customary language of the Reformés. In contrast with the satire of old-fashioned Catholic teachers and practices in chapters 14 and 17-21, Ponocrates substitutes study of 'quelque pagine de la divine Escripture', midday grace in the form of Reformed 'canticques' rather than Catholic 'hymnes', evening prayer emphasizing faith in the 'divine clemence' of 'Dieu le createur' rather than intercession of saints, and attendance at 'concions des prescheurs evangeliques' (2, pp. 88, 90, 96-97 and 98). If the assumption be accepted that *Gargantua* 23-24 and *Pantagruel* 8 are basically serious, it would seem also possible to accept the assessment of Rabelais's religious position, at least at the time of these two books, as a moderate Evangelicalism of the type of Erasmus.[13]

One other pervasive element is that of friendly and enjoyable companionship: Ponocrates even 'pour les premiers jours ... tolera' Gargantua as he first found him (ch. 23, 2, p.87). Later 'tout leur jeu

---

[13] This is the view put forward by Febvre (*23*), Lebègue ('Rabelais, the last of the French Erasmians', *Journal of the Warburg and Courtauld Institutes*, XI (1949)), Saulnier (*39*) and Screech (*41* and *42*), and shared by Telle (*BHR*, XIX (1957), pp.208-33), Levi (*RG*, pp.71-85), Sutherland (*RG*, pp.13-38) and Duval (*22*; see also his article on *Pantagruel* 8 in *RIB*).

n'estoit qu'en liberté', and the chapters continue to sparkle with words such as 'plaisoit', 'doulcement', 'joyeusement', 'plaisantement', 'se esbaudissoient', 'à son plaisir', 'faisans grand chere', 'faire la plus grande chère dont ilz se pouvoient adviser'. Perhaps, among modern critics, Glauser (25, pp.196-203) best renders the feeling of exuberant enjoyment of the universe resulting from Ponocrates's education. Few of Rabelais's ideas may have been new in 1534, and some may be dubious; but he has bequeathed to his readers unforgettable imaginative symbols.

5. Friendship: Pantagruel 9-22

Into the story-line of *Pantagruel* and the life of the hero irrupts the irrepressible Panurge, 'the man ready to do anything', or, as Screech calls him, 'craftiness personified' (*41*, p.70). Gargantua has no similar friend in *Les Grandes et Inestimables Cronicques*, where Merlin is his tutor and only companion; but that a striking figure should emerge from an anonymous crowd or the thick of battle to enter permanently into the hero's life is part of many literary traditions, as indeed of reality. Panurge, however, is no David to Pantagruel's Jonathan, still less an Oliver to his Roland. Countless attempts have been made to characterize Panurge and to determine why Pantagruel should accept him into his circle, or rather, avoiding the temptation to think of characters as real people, why Rabelais, creating such a character, should allow him to be accepted by his other creations.

Breathtaking are Panurge's gaiety, imagination, charm and impudence; his infinite capacity for cunning, mystification and surprise; his gift of the gab and of blarney; his sense of artistry and drama, timing and the fit degree of overstatement or understatement; his self-confidence, cruelty, treachery, bad taste and filthy speech. He has been derived, according to critics, from the classical Hermes (L. Schrader, *Panurge und Hermes*, Bonn (1958)) and Ulysses (Defaux, *19*); from the mediaeval Renart (Lote, *33*, p.366) and Pathelin (Plattard, *34*, p.69); from the François Villon of legend rather than of history (*33*, pp.366-67); and from Italian sources (*34*, pp.21-23). Griffin (*Studi Francesi*, XVI (1972); pp.329-36), Defaux (*18*, pp.173-74 and 185-86) and La Charité (*30*, pp.24 and 82-83) see him as the Devil; Vachon (*47*, p.131) and Defaux (*18*, pp.152-56) as Pantagruel's complement or other half; Lonigan (*Studi Francesi*, VIII (1964), p.275) as the other half of Rabelais himself. Further problems are posed by his evolution in the later books into an irresolute and superstitious coward; but he is complex enough in *Pantagruel*, where his prayers in chapter 14 contrast with blasphemies in 16-17 and 22, and his fear in ch. 21 with courage in 24-25 and 29. Dorothy Coleman (*16*, p.150), Carol Clark (*15*, pp.125-33) and John Parkin (*RG*, p.128) wisely emphasize that he is a central figure for comic episodes and 'turns' in which his reactions may well be different and inconsistent.

In chapter 9 he introduces himself to the prince by begging-speeches in thirteen different languages, apart from French, including three long thought to have been invented by Rabelais. The latest of several attempts to identify them is that of P. Vassal (*BARD*, III, vi-viii (1977-9), pp.250-51, 313-14 and 352-54): speech 2, he says, could be Hispano-Arabic, speech 6 bad Swedish[14] and the penultimate speech a second type of Greek, poetic and rhetorical. Critics see subtleties in the scene varying with their own linguistic stance. According to Gray (*26*, pp.44-45), Bastiaensen (*Revue belge*, LII (1974), pp.544-65) and Cave (*The Cornucopian Text*, Oxford (1979), p.115) Panurge is trying every possible approach because Pantagruel cannot or will not understand facts which speak for themselves. According to Spitzer (*44*, pp.411-12), Dorothy Coleman (*16*, p.153), Rigolot (*36*, pp.35-37), Armine Kotin (*Modern Language Notes*, XCII (1977), pp.691-709) and Defaux (*19*, p.27) it is Panurge who 'hinders communication', enjoying his own ingenuity at the expense of Pantagruel and his companions.

However, it is surely evident from the start that Panurge and Pantagruel are playing with each other on equal terms. From Pantagruel's first questions Panurge knows that Pantagruel will understand French, and ten lines later Pantagruel knows that Panurge understands it, from his literal obedience to the instruction 'parlez aultre langaige' (*2*, p.264). They are like good fencers or tennis-players keeping up a long rally; every new show of virtuosity by Panurge is parried by Pantagruel in a new way, forcing Panurge to attack from a new angle; parried, one should rather say, by

---

[14] In the 1542 edition, by which date four of Panurge's speeches, including this one, have been added.

Pantagruel or by one of his companions, so that Panurge has to fight
alone against four. It is his endurance, versatility, humour and
readiness to continue the game of incomprehension even when
Epistemon and Carpalim have dropped out and admitted that they
understand (2, p.268), which initially endear Panurge to Pantagruel.
'Je vous ay ja prins en amour si grand que, si vous condescendez à
mon vouloir, vous ne bougerez jamais de ma compaignie', says the
latter, and Panurge replies in kind, 'je accepte voluntiers l'offre,
protestant jamais ne vous laisser, et alissiez vous à tous les diables'
(2, pp.269-70). Pantagruel's later promise, 'je te veulx habiller de ma
livree' (ch. 15, 2, p.299, seen by La Charité as the critical moment of
the book, *30*, pp.93-115), promotes Panurge no higher than before; it
merely tidies up the loose end left by chapter 9's description of
Panurge's rags (as chapter 14 attends to his thirst) and permits a
transition to the subject of his *braguette*, which will recur in later
chapters.

The exploits of Panurge now alternate or combine with continuing exploits by Pantagruel himself. In chapter 10 Pantagruel
announces his readiness to maintain in public debate 760 different
contentions (9764 from 1537 onwards, 2, p.271), parodying a real
custom of the time but perhaps particularly the offer of Pico della
Mirandola in 1486 (mentioned inaccurately by Thaumaste in ch. 18,
2, p.314) to sustain 900 theses in Rome. Pantagruel defeats all the
members of the Paris Faculties of Arts and Theology, and all or 'la
plus part' of the doctors and Church lawyers (at whom Rabelais is
laughing rather than at Pantagruel, *pace* Brault, *12*, pp.620-21 and
630).

In chapters 10-13 he hears and settles a lawsuit which has for
nearly a year nonplussed the most expert lawyers of three countries
(see *10*, pp.146-50, and *11*, II, pp.220-354). His emphasis, like that
of Ponocrates in *Gargantua* 23-24, is on first-hand viva voce discussion and return to classical texts and basic principles, 'equité
evangelicque' (2, p.275). Pantagruel's nonsense in reply to the
plaintiff's and defendant's nonsense is a comic illustration of the
proverb *à sotte demande, sotte réponse*; but, more than that, Pantagruel reconciles them in their own terms 'par un geste géant de

sociabilité' (Rigolot, *36*, p.48; cf. Screech, *41*, pp.76-86, and Parkin, *ER* XVIII (1985), pp.65-69). The satirical sting lies in his comment (ch. 13, *2*, p.285) that certain ancient laws are still more incomprehensible than this case, and in Rabelais's adding in 1537 (*2*, p.287) that no lawsuit since the Flood had ever been settled so happily. Pantagruel's refusal in chapter 14 of the office of deputy judge or even supreme judge in the High Court is no sudden conversion, as Defaux holds (*18*, pp.145-52); it is quite consistent with his views on law expressed in chapter 10 and indeed chapter 5, and with Gargantua's quotation from mediaeval church tradition, 'science sans conscience n'est que ruine de l'ame' (*Pantagruel* 8, 2, pp.261-62; see Busson, *14*).

The remainder of chapter 14 and chapter 15 feature again Panurge's gift of the gab; if he is to be believed, he has recently paralleled Pantagruel's victories by destroying and escaping from a townful of Turks, traditional enemies of Christendom since the time of the crusade epics. His story of the lion, the fox and the old woman (on which see especially *36*, pp.116-19, and *30*, pp.93-115), or at least one element in it, may have been called to Rabelais's mind by the passage in *Les Grandes et Inestimables Cronicques* where Grant Gosier is attracted to Galemelle 'car ilz estoyent tous nudz'. Panurge's ingenuity, free from all scruples of morality, decency or respect, is seen in action in chapters 16-17, where his linguistic parodies are also to be noticed: parody of scholastic language, 'comme dit *De Alliaco*'; of courtly compliment, 'vostre noble cueur'; of fashion terms, 'propos de lingerie'; of musical terms, 'contrepoint de la musique'; of Latin, '*grates vobis, Dominos*'; of the Bible, '*centuplum accipies*'; of legal language, 'presentay requeste'; and of language itself, 'fretinfretailler'. The parody of *courtoisie* will reappear in chapters 21-22, alternating with the crudest obscenity of word and deed (see *15*, pp.127-28, and Parkin, *RG*, pp.129-35).

Perhaps Panurge can be charged, at least loosely, with sadism; but can Rabelais? There is certainly no evidence that he got any sexual stimulus out of infliction of pain or description of it, nor that he intended or expected his readers to get any. In fact, pain plays little part in his books; even in Panurge's tall tale in chapter 14, a larger role is played by fear. What interests Rabelais more than either pain or fear is either comic humiliation of the custard-pie sort, or destruction so rapid and complete that it would be virtually pain-less even if inflicted on sentient beings. But it is not so inflicted; Rabelais sees to it that his imagined victims (other than culpable villains) are from the start desensitized by conventionalization and exaggeration, mere puppets incapable of true feeling like the lady prepared to 's'escrier ... non trop hault' (2, p.331), or statistics impossible to believe like the drowned Parisians, 'deux cens soixante mille quatre cens dix et huyt, sans les femmes et petiz enfans' (2, 68). Admittedly Rabelais gives expression, under control, to aggres-sive impulses; but how many novels or games do not do the same? Compared with many present-day thriller-writers, Rabelais is about as sadistic as a chess-player. As for Panurge, Rabelais uses his narrator to make mild protests (2, pp.308 and 311), and will dissoci-ate himself from Panurge still more in books III and IV; but in this book he has set himself to bring us under Panurge's spell until we agree with Pantagruel, who 'prenoit à tout plaisir' (ch. 31, 2, p.376).

Chapters 18-20 show Pantagruel and Panurge in alliance against the foreigner Thaumaste. His name means 'magician or wonder-worker' (41, p.89), but has overtones of Thomas, the tradi-tional French nickname for an Englishman (41, p.90). To make him a native of England, the political and cultural would-be rival of France, and thought much inferior by the latter, would have an extra sting; but Anglophobe satire is not the main point. The story is one more example, with subtle implications, of Panurge's getting himself into a tight corner and out of it again. The tale of the stranger who comes to test the world-famous expert has Biblical and classical forms, mentioned by Thaumaste himself (2, pp.313-14). The motif of the servant standing in for the master has also folktale analogues, the most obvious being David's championing Saul against Goliath (I Sam. XVII).

The idea of a dispute by signs alone is based on a story told by the thirteenth-century lawyer Accursius (see 41, p.89). Communica-tion by signs, though not often by signs alone, was (41, pp.87-88) and is of course a real-life possibility; but Panurge's signs, described in elaborate quasi-medical terms, turn out to be nose-thumbing and worse. The signs appear to signify to Thaumaste something quite other than what they signify unmistakably to the reader. As for the other experts present, they are evidently in the position of the courtiers of Hans Andersen's emperor without clothes. Rabelais's main satire is certainly against the gullibility of those whose learning blinds them to real life. Screech (*41*, pp.90-96) may be right in seeing still deeper levels of satire against superstitious connoisseurs of miracles, magic and occult knowledge; although Parkin (*ER*, XVIII (1985), pp. 69-82) argues that the elements of satire are outweighed by those of parody.

Enough has been said to illustrate the complexity of Panurge; but are his attractive and amusing qualities sufficient to justify his place in the plot and in Pantagruel's heart? Krailsheimer (*29*, p.57) sees Pantagruel in chapter 9 as impelled by a 'mouvement absolument désintéressé de charité'; Glauser (*25*, p.36) compares Panurge's attraction for Pantagruel with La Boétie's indefinable one for Montaigne, 'par ce que c'estoit luy: par ce que c'estoit moy' (*Les Essais*, ed. Villey and Saulnier, Paris (1965), I, 28, p.188). Panurge, of course, does not displace Pantagruel's other friends. The giant comes to be surrounded by a group of favoured and congenial paladins, moral and physical exemplars as Panurge exemplifies mental skill: in chapter 5 Epistemon; in chapter 9 Carpalim, Eusthenes (from 1534) and Eudemon (in 1542, jumping the generation-gap); and, in the Prologue and chapters 17 and 32, although only in a very limited sense offered as an exemplar, the narrator himself (see *16*, chs. 3 and 4, and *37*, pp.145-47).

Around Gargantua a similar circle forms. Ponocrates and Eudemon go to Paris with him at the end of chapter 15; but he needs more companions, Anagnostes, Gymnaste and Rhizotome, for the five-part singing and physical exercises of chapter 23. Ponocrates, Eudemon and, most of all, Gymnaste are given predominance in the war against Picrochole, and all three are rewarded in chapter 51. And into Gargantua's group, as into Pantagruel's, irrupts an exciting and explosive character: Frère Jean.

Like Panurge, he has no analogue in *Les Grandes et Inestimables Cronicques*; his role and function in *Gargantua* partially reflect those of Panurge in *Pantagruel*. His portrait is painted in *Gargantua* 27 very much as is Panurge's in *Pantagruel* 16. He is shown in action in *Gargantua* 27 as Panurge is in *Pantagruel* 9. In *Gargantua* 39-41 he is welcomed into the circle of royal favourites, as Panurge is welcomed by Pantagruel. Gargantua is first attracted to Frère Jean (*Gargantua* 39, 2, p.146) by hearing of his defence of his monastery against enemy attack, the action which we have earlier been shown directly.

With boundless courage, energy and gusto, charm and humour, and with piety of a sort, Frère Jean has his imperfections, as Panurge has. He turns out to be Rabelais's ideal monk only in that he discards and reverses the accepted monastic ideal. 'Il n'est point bigot,' says Gargantua in chapter 40 (2, p.153), 'il n'est poinct dessiré' (*déchiré*, ragged; Jean takes care of his appearance, as Eudemon does, ch. 14). 'Il travaille; il labeure;' continues Gargantua, 'il defent les opprimez; il conforte les affligez; il subvient es souffreteux; il garde les clous de l'abbaye'. But the 'defence' is by unscrupulous slaughter, and the 'work', Jean adds comically, includes making crossbow-bolts and rabbit-snares while reciting his offices. Like Panurge, Jean can be charged with both cruelty and presumption, over-confidence in himself, as he is by Demerson (in *ER*, XXI, pp.228-29); but, again, Rabelais endows him with enough charm to outweigh such a charge, 'un certain héroïsme de l'action terrestre' (Demerson, ib.).

Chapter 27 (2, p.107) called him 'bien fendu de gueule, bien advantaigé en nez, beau despecheur d'heures', a good eater and drinker, sexy and speedy at rattling through his recitations; and though the description concludes by calling him 'clerc jusques es dents', he himself boasts absurdly, 'Je n'estudie poinct, de ma part. En nostre abbaye nous ne estudions jamais, de peur des auripeaux' (ch. 39, 2, pp.149-50). Carefree and ignorant (though less ignorant than he claims), he reverses not only the monastic ideal but several Renaissance ideals; his speech in defence of *boyre matin* (ch. 41, 2, p.155) is very like that of the unregenerate Gargantua in chapter 21 (2, p.81). If Gargantua symbolizes the coming of the Renaissance (see p.13 above), Frère Jean, like Grandgousier, represents, and would have held much appeal for, those who watched it with genial approval but without full participation. His natural, easy familiarity can manage without it.

Like Panurge, Frère Jean takes an important share in his prince's war; and victory brings a special reward to each, to Jean the Abbaye de Theleme, to Panurge in chapter 30 a royal prisoner (*2*, p.373; the estate of Salmigondin is not Panurge's until later, *Tiers Livre*, ch. 2, *2*, p.410). From the *Tiers Livre* onwards, when Gargantua drops out of the action, Frère Jean and Panurge become equally the companions and friends of Pantagruel. The radical difference and opposition between their two characters sharpens: Panurge becomes more and more cowardly in contrast with Jean's courage, and Jean more moral and wise in contrast with Panurge's irresponsibility. Yet Pantagruel never loses his affection for Panurge.

Loyal friendship and happy companionship seem to have been of great importance to Rabelais, as to his giants. There is little evidence that he had one close friend like Montaigne's La Boétie, unless it was Pierre Amy or Lamy in his monastery years; but there is certainly evidence that he found himself at home in merry 'Pantagruelizing' circles, in Poitiers, Paris, Lyons and Rome. Pantagruelism, the imagined philosophy, named after Pantagruel, which Rabelais advertised on the title-page of *Gargantua*, is no metaphysical chain of doctrines (see especially *39*, I, pp.23-27 and 43-56; *28*, p.307; and *29*, pp.76-80). 'Estre bons Pantagruelistes' is defined by Rabelais from 1534 onwards as 'vivre en paix, joye, santé, faisans tousjours grande chere' (*Pantagruel* 34, *2*, p.387); 'Pantagruelisant' as 'beuvans à gré et lisans les gestes horrificques de Pantagruel' (*Gargantua* 1, *2*, p.13). Pantagruelism will develop into what Emile Faguet summed up as a 'stoïcisme gai' (*Seizième Siècle*, Paris (1894), p.100): Pantagruelists 'jamais en maulvaise partie ne prendront choses quelconques ilz congnoistront sourdre de bon, franc et loyal couraige' (*Tiers Livre*, Prologue); Pantagruelism is 'certaine gayeté d'esprit conficte en mespris des choses fortuites' (*Quart Livre*, Prologue of 1552). But it is never an egoistic isolationism.

One of Pantagruel's chief concerns wherever he goes is to find 'joyeuse compagnie' (*Pantagruel* 5, 2, p.241, and cf. pp.239, 242 and 243), and Rabelais aims to establish a similar relationship between himself and his readers (*Gargantua*, Prologue, 2, p.9). The counsels in Gargantua's letter to his son include 'Soys serviable à tous tes prochains, et les ayme comme toymesmes', 'conversant entre gens de honneur et ... amys' (*Pantagruel* 8, 2, pp.262 and 257). The climax of both the chapters on Gargantua's re-education is the enjoyment of merry companionship. Feasting celebrates Pantagruel's victories over Anarche (*Pantagruel* 25-26 and 30-31) and Gargantua's over Picrochole (*Gargantua* 37-40, 45 and 51). We shall find friendship to be one of the great principles, perhaps the most basic, of the Abbaye de Theleme; and when Pantagruel's ship is becalmed in the *Quart Livre* (chs. 63-64; see *39*, II, pp.132-41; *41*, pp.450-55; and T. Cave, *The Cornucopian Text*, Oxford (1979), pp.215-22), and when Panurge comes to the end of his quest in the *Quint Livre* (if chapters 45-46 are to any extent by Rabelais), a friendly banquet turns out to be the solution of all problems.

A good Pantagruelist, Rabelais seems to be saying in *Pantagruel* 9 and throughout his books, is always ready generously to extend the hand of friendship.

6. *War: Pantagruel 23-29 and Gargantua 25-49*

It may seem supremely absurd to call Rabelais's treatment of war realistic; for some readers it is not even acceptably comic. But realism is not necessarily the point-by-point record of a naïve photographer, and its opposite is not necessarily a culpable failure to achieve realism. Other opposites are symmetrical pattern-making, idealization or grotesque uglification, understatement or exaggeration, parody, fantasy or deliberate inconsistency, all of which Rabelais practises on different occasions. Yet there is in Rabelais, and in all the best writers even of fantasy, a deeper realism to which one responds, 'Yes, I see that that could or would follow in the universe this author has created', together with an ethical realism which one recognizes as echoing one's own scale of values or a universal scale. It is the chronicles of Gargantua, not Rabelais's books, which indulge in the sheer escapism for which anything may happen and might is right. Further, it is when causative and ethical realism are achieved that a story of war can, even to pacifists, be acceptable and, if humorously presented, amusing.

Rabelais's suggestions about politics, the science and art of government, and especially about war, the prominent mediaeval and Renaissance form of foreign policy, have often been set out with competent clarity.[15] This does not mean, however, that Rabelais can be accused of having over-simple views. He has simplified issues for the purpose of his stories, loading the dice to make his points; black is jet-black, white is not only snow-white but ultimately successful.

---

[15] See *33*, pp.265-80; H. Janeau, *FR*, pp.20-35; *31*, pp.345-61; N. Aronson, *Les Idées Politiques de Rabelais*, Paris, 1973; F.-M. Plaisant, *Bull. de l'Assocn. Guillaume Budé*, XXXIII (1974), pp.467-92; E. Benson, *ER*, XIII (1976), pp.147-61; and R.M. Berrong, *Every Man for Himself: Social Order and its Dissolution in Rabelais*, Saratoga, 1985, ch. 1.

But by 1533 he had been accepted into the circle of the du Bellay brothers, a bishop-diplomat and a soldier-statesman, where conversation would not have been naïve. Even earlier, as a practising doctor, he must have learnt the danger of trying to apply simple and rigid rules either to a group of cases or to an individual case. As in the field of education, he offers principles for our consideration, suggests that they may work in appropriate forms in real life, leaves us to think about them, and meanwhile entertains us with science-fiction based on them.

Certainly his fiction is less simple than *Les Grandes et Inestimables Cronicques*. For that thriller of action and excitement, war is an obvious theme and way to make the most of a giant hero. Half the story is devoted to narrating how Gargantua defeated three attacks against King Arthur, the first apparently unprovoked, the second a refusal of tribute, the third in revenge for the failure of the other two. Despite Arthur's sobriquet of 'le bon roy', his only concession to his opponents is to send one embassy; his victories are followed by merciless slaughter, after which pillage is taken to be normal by the author. Rabelais goes much deeper than this; but it may not always be realized how far his views, to some extent equating with modern humanitarianism, were in his time unusual.

There was then no accepted code of international law, even if the Middle Ages had handed down some idea of 'natural law' and some systems of customary law. Most countries had no written constitution. There was next to no idea of democracy; almost all states were monarchies, and the few republics had a very limited franchise. War was the natural state of relations between nations; alliances, truces and peaces were occasional and temporary constructions. No one felt guilty about this: the education of a mediaeval or Renaissance aristocrat was for war; both the mediaeval chivalric code and the morality of the ancient Greeks and Romans (that fashionable study of Renaissance readers) saw war as an opportunity for showing virtues and winning glory. The Church defined and permitted the 'just war'; and the new efficiency-theory of Machiavelli declared: 'A wise prince ... has no other object and no other interest and takes as his profession nothing else than war' (*The*

Prince, ch. 14, tr. A. Gilbert, *Machiavelli, The Chief Works and Others*, Durham, N.C., 1965, p.55). The only promulgators of pacifist ideas were a few humanists such as More and Erasmus, both of whom patently influenced Rabelais, although he remained independent and eclectic in what he took from them.

Allusions in the texts make it clear that two great sixteenth-century movements were in Rabelais's mind as he wrote the later part of *Pantagruel* and the greater part of *Gargantua*. One was the competition between France and the Holy Roman Empire for domination in Europe. In Rabelais's youth the French had five or six times invaded Italy, the nearest and most tempting field for conquest and plunder. Several of the Italian states, not united by anything more than temporary alliances, were dependencies of the Empire, whose ruler Charles V, elected Emperor in 1519, was already by inheritance King of Spain, Naples and Sicily, and Archduke of the Netherlands. The outcome of this situation, before Rabelais's death, was to be six or seven further wars between François I and Charles. Rabelais, enough of a pacifist to hope for a stable 'balance of power', could still be enough of a French royalist to see the Emperor as the aggressor. It is François, defeated at Pavia and abandoned by fleeing followers (1525; *Gargantua* 39, 2, p.149), whom Rabelais represents as 'miserablement traicté, durement emprisonné et rançonné extremement' (*Gargantua* 50, 2, p.183).

The other great movement was the race to conquer and colonize outside Europe, in Rabelais's time chiefly a race between Spain and Portugal, although France and England were beginning to join in. More than any war in sixteenth-century Europe, this race threw up the problems of the rights and duties of conquerors and conquered, problems in Rabelais's thoughts in both books, and still when he began the *Tiers Livre*. Pantagruel, according to Rabelais's forecast, 'naviga par la mer Athlanticque, et deffit les caniballes, et conquesta les isles de Perlas' (in the West Indies; *Pantagruel* 34, 2, p.385). Grandgousier was able to establish more friendly relations with the Canary Islands (*Gargantua* 13, 2, p.54, but also 50, 2, pp.182-83) and with 'Spagnola' (Haiti, 50, 2, p.182, including the Spanish settlement of Isabella, 31, 2, p.118). The book-title in the library of Saint-Victor, 'L'Entree de Anthoine de Leive es Terres du Bresil' (*Pantagruel* 7, 2, p.252, added in 1537), unites the two themes of colonization and European competition; the suggestion is that when Charles V's commander Antonio de Leyva invaded Provence in 1536 he treated the inhabitants as conquered savages.

In Rabelais's mind, thirdly, was doubtless a long-standing quarrel and lawsuit over water-rights between his own father and a next-door neighbour, Gaucher de Sainte-Marthe. One cannot go all the way with Lefranc (*1*, I, pp.lx-lxxii) in seeing *Gargantua* 25-50 as a satire specifically directed against Sainte-Marthe; but the quarrel may have suggested to Rabelais the idea of localizing the warfare in ten or twelve square miles of the Loire valley, with place-names, directions and distances exactly reproduced. The absurdity of situating international hostilities in such a tiny area would simultaneously satirize Sainte-Marthe by inflating him to the size of an epic hero, and kings and emperors by reducing their exploits to microscopic scale.

Rabelais shows us two bad kings of different types. Anarche is the non-king, the man unfit to be king, the man with no sense of right rule, the complete opposite of a Renaissance monarch expected to preside over his own council of war, as well as being the ultimate authority over peace-time institutions. Anarche is not even heard of until the middle of chapter 26; he plays no part in any of the military action. It is with more docility than either courage or prudence that he swallows the thirst-provoking drug sent by his opponent; and he submits with the same docility to his treatment by Panurge and by his own bride in chapter 31. The motif of his followers' drunken disorderliness runs through *Pantagruel* 26-29 (*2*, pp.348, 355-57, 360), just as the theme of the unbridled rage of Picrochole and his followers recurs from *Gargantua* 25 onwards.

Picrochole is the man of picric choler, a compound term in medical use signifying bitter anger (*6*, p.271 and *41*, p.164), with no control over his own emotions. At a biased report of a frontier incident (ch. 25) he conscripts both those normally liable for military service and the reserves ('ban et arriere ban', ch. 26, 2, p.104), with the death-penalty for draft-dodgers ('sur peine de la hart'), with no investigation of the situation ('sans plus oultre se interroguer quoy ne comment') and with a casual disregard of the importance of his measures ('en disnant'). His army lays everything waste ('sans ordre et mesure', 2, p.105), with no declaration of war, no reason given and no attention to remonstrances, 'sinon qu'ilz leurs vouloient aprendre à manger de la fouace'. Picrochole treats Grandgousier's herald with complete discourtesy (ch. 30, 2, p.117), disregards his deeply-thought and very reasonable speech (ch. 31), treats concessions as a sign of weakness: 'Ces rustres ont belle paour ... Saisissez ce qu'ilz ont amené' (ch. 31, 2, pp.123-24), and lets his courtiers launch him into the fantastical dream of world-conquest of chapter 33. (It is based on Plutarch and Lucian, but updated and extravagantly enriched; see *36*, pp.133-36.) Future tenses become perfects and preterites unnoticed by any of the characters, Picrochole has forgotten by the end of the chapter that he is supposed to have defeated Grandgousier at the beginning, and an alliance with Russia is seen as the solution of all problems.

The good ruler is represented in *Pantagruel* by that hero alone, since Gargantua has been 'translaté au pays des Phées par Morgue' (ch. 23, 2, p.335), a borrowing from the end of *Les Grandes et Inestimables Cronicques* inserted with ostentatious perfunctoriness. He is represented in *Gargantua* by both the prince and his father, the portrait of the latter in chapter 28 being made initially comic, in order to make human and acceptable his touching soliloquy there and, in the next chapter, his reasonable letter to his son (however Ciceronian in style it may be; see the arguments of Brault, *12*, and the counter-arguments of ch. 4 above, pp.37-38).

Embedded in chapters 28 and 29 are almost all the elements of Rabelais's ideal of monarchy. A state exists by the 'droict naturel' (2, p.115) of its hereditary monarch, willingly supported by those whom he willingly protects, both his own 'pauvres subjectz' (2, p.114) and allied states ('je l'ay secouru', 2, p.113). His duty, if attacked, is first to seek the help of God ('mon Dieu, mon Saulveur', ib.) and of his own 'conseil' (2, p.114); then to enquire through 'quelque homme prudent' (ib.), negotiate and offer compensation (2, p.115); finally to resort to arms, 'vertus' in the Latin sense of military valour (ib.); but still to hope for the conversion of the enemy 'par bonne discipline' (2, p.114) and to prefer 'ruzes de guerre' to bloodshed (2, p.116). It is not quite clear whether Grandgousier's concern is to spare the lives[16] of his own men alone or the enemy's too; Gargantua, as well as Frère Jean and Panurge, inflicts heavy casualties; but certainly the close of each war reconciles both sides and sends both alike 'joyeux à leurs domiciles' (ib.).

Grandgousier, as can be seen, is not a complete pacifist. There is a section of his people which responds to invasion by complete non-resistance: 'ne luy feut faicte resistance quelconques' (ch. 28, 2, p.112), 'un chascun se mettoit à leur mercy' (ch. 26, 2, p.105). Rabelais represents this attitude respectfully and nobly, not as fear or apathy but as reasoned surrender to the will of God: 'Dieu les en puniroit' (ib.). However, in chapter 27 Rabelais ridicules the similar pacifism of the monks of Seuillé, perhaps because it includes elements of ignorance and superstition, perhaps thinking that farm-labourers cannot be expected to fight but well-born able-bodied men should not be monks. To the scrimshankers of Seuillé Rabelais prefers the glorious rumbustiousness of Frère Jean. (On ch. 27 see R.A. Sayce, *Style in French Prose*, Oxford, 1953, *passim*; A. Gendre, *Mélanges offerts à Carl Theodor Gossen*, Bern, 1976, pp.239-75; and *41*, pp.170-84).

Jean blows away mental cobwebs as he blows away Picrochole's army: 'les heures sont faictez pour l'homme, et non l'homme pour les heures' (ch. 41, 2, p.156); 'je sçay quelque oraison ... mais elle ne me profitera de rien, car je n'y adjouste poinct de foy' (ch. 42, 2, p.157). In the same way Panurge is at his best on active service, boastful ('tout seul les desconfiray', *Pantagruel* 25, 2, p.343) but living up to his boasts; treacherous to the enemy ('Nous nous rendons à vostre bon plaisir', 2, p.344) but never disloyal to his own side; encouraging Pantagruel when he falters ('Vous avez ... plus de

---

[16] 'Nous saulverons toutes les ames' (ch. 29, 2, p.116) is more likely to refer to the saving of lives than to the saving of souls; although chs. 40 and 45 (see *41*, pp.176-84 and 184-86) show Grandgousier's and Gargantua's concern for the religious beliefs of their subjects, like Pantagruel's concern in *Pantagruel* 29. (*Gargantua* 38, however, is nothing but a joke.)

force ... que n'eut jamais Hercules ...', ch. 29, 2, p.359) and, when he relaxes, bringing him back to the point ('Il vault mieulx penser de nostre affaire', ch. 26, 2, p.347). Both he and Jean are merciless, Jean even when asked for mercy (*Gargantua* 27, 2, p.110); his very name, Jean des Entommeures, is not, as so often rendered, John of the Funnels, but Jean des Entamures, John of the Slashes (*1*, II, p.260).

It appears that Rabelais advocates neither pacifism nor any 'golden mean'. He recommends two courses well to right and left of centre: for a fighting man, militarism which yet falls short of Picrochole's unprovoked and uncontrolled aggression; for a monarch, pacifism which yet falls short of the pacifism of the monks of Seuillé. Jean's and Panurge's readiness to retaliate, like that of the shepherds in *Gargantua* 25, imperils only themselves; a monarch who practised it would imperil his whole country. In politics, as elsewhere, Rabelais recommends not moderation or compromise, but a common sense which adapts itself to one's role and one's circumstances.

Common sense is seen also in Gargantua's conduct of his war (which it will be convenient to treat before Pantagruel's), and its opposite in the conduct of his opponents. (A map is available in *1*, I, between pp. lxxiv and lxxv.) Rabelais makes the tiny village of Lerné into Picrochole's capital; the town for which his bakers were bound is presumably Chinon, some seven miles away by road. Picrochole invades from the west to make his headquarters at La Roche-Clermault, a little more than half-way to Chinon. Rashly, he by-passes the farm of La Devinière, Rabelais's birthplace and evidently Grandgousier's palace; fortunately for him, Grandgousier is too peaceable to seize the opportunity of cutting the invading force in two. Gargantua comes to the rescue from the north-east, using his initiative with admirable skill: he bases himself on La Vauguyon, half-way between Chinon and La Roche-Clermault, and sends out a reconnaissance party (Gymnaste and Prelinguand, chapters 34 and 35) whose report makes possible the victory at the ford of Vède (chapter 36) and Gargantua's safe arrival at La Devinière. The Picrocholean survivors flee, not vaguely 'vers les cousteaux à gauche' (2, p.137), but precisely to the village of Les Coteaux on

Gargantua's left flank, whence they can easily reach La Roche-Clermault.

Gargantua follows up his success with a second battle, which may be called also the second Battle of Seuillé, the night attack of chapter 41. An efficient force of fifty or fifty-five (2, p.157), well rested, well fed and suitably armed, is led by Gargantua in person and four friends, including the newly recruited Frère Jean. They meet Tyravant's absurdly large scouting-party of sixteen hundred (ch. 43, 2, p.160), who, armed with stoles and holy water, have wasted time and energy searching ridiculously far to the north-east (La Maladrerie) and south (Le Coudray) and taking captive five harmless pilgrims. At Jean's first call for a charge, the Picrocholeans flee in panic; Gargantua having ordered a halt because 'jamais ne fault mettre son ennemy en lieu de desespoir' (2, p.161), they believe Jean to be alone, capture him, leave him inadequately guarded and come on again. They are cut to pieces, and Picrochole's Master of Horse, Toucquedillon, is taken prisoner.

In chapter 46 Grandgousier interrogates him, not improperly, on Picrochole's war-aims; convinces him, by gentle and sound argument based on the Bible, Plato and Erasmus (see *41*, p.175), that a civil war 'n'est que superficiaire, elle n'entre poinct au profond cabinet de noz cueurs' (2, p.171) and need not proceed to extremes or for ever; and offers him a free choice of his future course. He is sufficiently impressed to ask for Grandgousier's own advice, which is, rather surprisingly, to remain loyal to his own king — and presumably to pass on to him Grandgousier's persuasions. This Toucquedillon tries to do in chapter 47; but he too comes of the nation of bitter anger. Accused of defection, he stabs his accuser, and is immediately executed without trial or mercy. The result is a drop in the morale of Picrochole's army ('plusieurs commencerent murmurer', 2, p.177); it is also running out of supplies, in spite of having suffered heavy casualties ('sommes icy mal pourveuz de vivres, et jà beaucoup diminuez en nombre'; 2, ib., misprints 'là beaucoup').

Gargantua has meanwhile called up his father's standing army ('les legions, lesquelles entretenoit ordinairement', 2, p.175), and in chapter 48 storms La Roche-Clermault from the north-west, while Frère Jean makes a quick circuit ('en grande diligence', 2, p.178) to the Loudun road and attacks from the east ('tyra vers le fort', 2, p.179). The town surrenders and Picrochole's troops flee in all directions ('en tous endroictz', 2, p.180). Cut off from home, he himself escapes, skirting Chinon, to Lyons, where like one of Molière's protagonists he lives on, 'cholere comme davant' (ch. 49, 2, p.181).

It may seem in comparison that Pantagruel's war is a fantastical medley of unrelated incidents. The boasts of his companions in chapters 24 and 26 are not followed up; anything may divert him and them from their aim, a love-affair (chapter 24), a banquet (26), the construction of a trophy[17] or the creation of a race of pygmies (27); and the fighting, when it does take place, is on totally unrealistic lines. Rabelais's aim is to make the chapbook Gargantua's exploits more interesting and entertaining, not by adding realism and depth as he will in his own *Gargantua*, but by inflating the style and diversifying the matter with the help of classical and other literary borrowings adapted or parodied. (See *16*, pp.93-96, and *46*, ch. 3.)

While chapter 23 takes from Greek the names of Utopia, the Dipsodes and the Amaurotes, Pantagruel's sudden departure is modelled on those of Arthurian knights, and the tale of Pharamond parallels those of 'first inventors' to be found in Renaissance encyclopaedias such as Polydore Vergil's *De Inventoribus Rerum* (1499). Chapter 24 demonstrates Panurge's and Rabelais's own encyclopaedic knowledge about invisible writing, though the letter to Pantagruel finally turns out to be one more example of communication by signs, turning on a pun and a twisted quotation from the New Testament engraved on a ring. (There is an Italian source; see P. Toldo, *Revue d'Hist. Litt. de la France*, XI (1904), pp.467-68.) Pantagruel sails round Africa before striking out into the Indian Ocean, by a route much discussed by critics seeking to situate

---

[17] See F. Joukovsky, *La Gloire dans la poésie française ... du XVIᵉ siècle*, Geneva, 1969, pp.391 ff., on classical and Renaissance trophies, scarecrow-like structures hung with enemy arms in derision, thanksgiving or sympathetic magic.

Rabelais's Utopia (see Lefranc, *Les Navigations de Pantagruel*, Paris, 1905, and Françon, *Mod. Lang. Notes*, LXIX (1954), pp.260-64). The symmetrical boasts which end chapter 24 derive from the folktale motif of gifts made to the hero himself; the story of Zopyrus comes from Herodotus via Erasmus, those of Sinon and Camilla from the *Aeneid*.

Carpalim's hunting achievements (ch. 26, 2, pp.345-46) are modelled on Aeneas's shooting seven stags in *Aen*. I, his raid on the enemy camp (ch. 28, 2, p.357) parodies that of Nisus and Euryalus in *Aen*. IX, and the classical and pseudo-classical trophies of chapter 27 have their parallel in *Aen*. XI. All these echoes serve to elevate Pantagruel into a mock-epic hero and commander-in-chief, who can go to war, in a triumph of Rabelais's surrealism, using as a walking-stick the mast of the ship he came in (ch. 28, 2, p.356).

The fanciful and perhaps amoral episodes of the actual fighting serve to entertain Rabelais's audience with amusing unexpectedness and incongruity. Some of the enemy had shown common sense in making the reconnaissance of chapter 25; they are defeated by a grotesque stratagem, coupled with shameless lying by Panurge ('Nous nous rendons à vostre bon plaisir', 2, p.344). The stratagem which immobilizes Anarche and his captains in chapter 28 is equally grotesque, and Pantagruel himself accompanies it with a false claim to military strength ('faignoit Pantagruel avoir armée sur mer') and a challenge which he has no intention of implementing ('demain sus le midy ... par dix huyt cens mille combatans et sept mille geans', 2, pp.353-54). Pantagruel's method of destroying the encamped enemies later in chapter 28 (2, p.358) is one which even the Gargantua of *Les Grandes et Inestimables Cronicques* did not use, though it will be imitated by the mare of Rabelais's Gargantua (*Gargantua* 36, 2, p.137). The pseudo-invocation which ends the chapter introduces in chapter 29 the climax of the war, Pantagruel's exaggeratedly melodramatic combat against Loup Garou, modelled simultaneously on Gargantua's combats in the *Cronicques* (where his weapon is a club, he throws a prisoner so high as to kill him, and he ends by killing a twelve-cubit giant) and on epic combats such as that of Aeneas and Turnus in *Aen*. XII.

Before that combat Aeneas had prayed and made vows for the future (XII, lines 176-94). Pantagruel does this during the duel itself, in a prayer even more fundamentally and consistently serious than chapter 8, and as unmistakeably Evangelical as Gargantua's second education. It has been much commented on by critics: see especially Febvre, *23*, pp.265 ff.; Krailsheimer, *29*, pp.38-41; Dorothy Coleman, *16*, pp.95 and 189-92; and Screech, *42*, pp.23-41 and *41*, pp.97-101. One should particularly note Screech's point that the succeeding 'voix du ciel', 'Hoc fac et vinces', echoes not only the vision of the Emperor Constantine, 'Hoc signo vinces' (*1*, IV, p.297; *2*, p.362; etc.) but also Luke X, 28, 'Hoc fac, et vives', where *hoc* refers to loving both God and one's neighbour. Pantagruel's vow to 'prescher ton sainct Evangile purement, simplement et entierement' (*2*, p.361) would be understood by Reformed readers as a promise to do both.

The depth, integrity and beauty of Pantagruel's prayer may seem at odds with the comic deceits he has just been practising. It is noteworthy that Gargantua and Frère Jean never deceive the enemy, although Gymnaste does ('je suys pauvre diable; je vous requiers qu'ayez de moy mercy', *2*, p.132). Perhaps Pantagruel's deceits, like those of Panurge and Gymnaste, count as legitimate 'ruzes de guerre', in *Gargantua* 29's phrase, against an unjustified aggressor; perhaps they are part of the inconsistency which Rabelais employs throughout *Pantagruel* in the service of parody and thought-provocation. Apart from these deceits, however, one can already see in Pantagruel the sound moral principles of Grandgousier and Gargantua. Like them, he takes for granted his duty to go immediately to the defence of his country and its people; like Grandgousier, he entrusts the success of his cause to the will of God. Like Gargantua, he delegates responsibility generously to his friends, co-operates with them in comradely fashion, and, at the point of crisis, puts at their service his resources of mind, body and spirit. In the two years or so between *Pantagruel* and *Gargantua* Rabelais did not change his views, whether on heroism, on realism or on war; only, after two years or so, he chose to put his views on war more explicitly and with a greater degree of his own type of realism.

7. *Victory, and Rabelais's Other Worlds: Pantagruel 30-33 and Gargantua 50-58*

Brusquely and flatly *Les Grandes et Inestimables Cronicques* drop all pretence of interest in what followed Gargantua's victory over Arthur's last enemy: 'Gargantua ... le porta tout mort a la court du Roy artus. Et ainsi vesquit Gargantua au service du Roy Artus lespace de deux cens ans troys moys et .iiii. jours justement. Puis fut porté en faierie par [Mor]gain la phee, et Melusine, avecques plusieurs aultres lesquelz y sont de present. FINIS.'

This is far from enough for the continually bubbling fantasy and endlessly questing imagination of Rabelais. Just as his sentences proceed by piling clause on clause, near-synonym on near-synonym, and then suddenly twist into an unexpected new development, so, on the vaster scale, his imagination proceeds by developing a situation logically to the point of the absurd and then abruptly, illogically, into a new dimension. We find it in *Gargantua* 20, where the completion of Janotus's embassy immediately involves him in two more disputes, one of which is unresolved 'encores ... jusques à present' (2, pp.78-79); we find it in *Pantagruel* 17, where the description of Panurge's ways and exploits suddenly introduces Rabelais — or at least Alcofribas — himself as a partner in them. Above all, the continuing realities borne in mind by Rabelais during his narration of Gargantua's war and to some extent even Pantagruel's, the fascinating discoveries and explorations of America, Southern Africa and the East Indies, and the ceaselessly self-renewing conflict between France and the Holy Roman Empire, leave his thought no resting-place; and by allusion, analogy or allegory, his work reflects these continuing processes.

There were wars enough in Rabelais's lifetime, but no conclusive or durable victories. Little footholds in Italy, won by the invasions of Charles VIII and Louis XII, were each lost after a few months or years. After François I's defeat at Pavia, French claims to Italy had to be renounced in the peace treaty of 1526. Rabelais was to witness new attempts by François in 1527, 1536-38 and 1542-44; but again the king would be forced to renounce his claims in treaties of 1529 and 1544.

Equally, there was no victory in France for Evangelical religious tendencies, whatever ground they had gained in German and Swiss states. If there was some relaxation of repression in France from 1531 to 1534, this was due to the oscillations of the policy of François I and his search for financial resources and foreign allies; but repression resumed to some extent in the spring of 1534, and much more in autumn 1534 and January 1535, after the *affaires des placards* (see p.8 above). The first trial of men accused of putting up the anti-Catholic posters resulted in seven death-sentences, and they were not the last. Screech (see p.10 above) has impressed some critics, but not yet all, with his arguments that *Gargantua* was not completed and published until after the first or even the second of these *affaires*; but whether it was earlier or later, Rabelais might well represent Gargantua as saying, 'Ce n'est de maintenant que les gens reduictz [ramenés] à la creance Evangelicque sont persecutez' (ch. 58, 2, p.209).

So Rabelais dreams — apocalyptically, Costa (*17*) would say — of other worlds, perhaps ideal, perhaps just thought-provokingly different, to be entered into after victory.

Of course he sees to it that Pantagruel and Gargantua make practical arrangements for the future of the kingdoms they have just defeated. Pantagruel has liberated his own town, always described as that of the Amaurotes (the Obscure, an apt name borrowed from More for the inhabitants of Utopia, Nowhere), and consequently the rest of his country. We are not invited to enter into the feelings of the beaten and humiliated Anarche, who remains docile and incompetent to the end; he is a carnival king as pictured by Bakhtin (*8*) and Parkin (*RG*, pp.125-39), whose fall provides amusement for Pantagruel as well as for Panurge, and who is treated by them with some liberality if not true generosity.

Rabelais lets Pantagruel annex Anarche's kingdom, but at least 'en ... bon ordre' (ch. 31, 2, p.375), in contrast with Picrochole's invasion 'sans ordre et mesure' (*Gargantua* 26, 2, p.105). Pantagruel brings the Dipsodian enemies friendship and good cheer, 'la main au pot et le verre au poing' (*Pantagruel* 32, 2, p.377); he has the excuse that Utopia is overpopulated ('ceste ville est tant pleine des habitans qu'ilz ne peuvent se tourner par les rues', 31, 2, p.374); and the majority of the Dipsodians welcome his orderly rule: 'tout le monde en estoit joyeux, et incontinent se rendirent à luy ... exceptez les Almyrodes ...' (32, 2, p.377; briefer in the first edition). Pantagruel has indeed by this time something of the paternal care of the God of the Bible; the image of chapter 32, 'les ... couvrit comme une geline faict ses poulletz', recalls Christ's words in Matthew XXIII, 37 and Luke XIII, 34.

Gargantua's peace terms, still more generous, are clearly set out in his speech to the defeated army in chapter 50, and in the short narrative chapter which follows. Supposed allusions to the past kindness of his house to the 'Bretons', the 'barbares de Spagnola' and the king of 'Canarre' (2, p.183) are offered as proof that clemency on the part of the conquerors results in the eternal and increasing gratitude of the conquered. Picrochole is taken to have abdicated, and his infant son is allowed to succeed him (2, p.185) under a regency. Rabelais may be accused on the one hand of over-idealism, on the other hand of the despotic setting up of a puppet government; but at least his suggestions are more liberal than the annexation with reprisals which was not rare in his time and is not unknown in ours.

The regent is to be Gargantua's own teacher and inspirer, Ponocrates, who evidently was not killed in chapter 49 but merely wounded. Richard Berrong (*ER*, XVIII (1985), p.42) argues for a resurrection of Ponocrates recalling that of Epistemon. But surely, in the sentence 'Gargantua premierement recensa les gens et trouva que peu d'iceulx estoient peryz en la bataille, sçavoir est quelques gens de pied de la bande du capitaine Tolmere, et Ponocrates qui avoit un coup de harquebouze en son pourpoinct' (2, p.181), 'Ponocrates' is not the complement of 'sçavoir est' (in the first edition, 'exceptez') but a second object of 'trouva'. If the sentence is somewhat sylleptical, it is no more so than Grandgousier's 'Picrochole, mon amy ancien de tout temps, de toute race ...' (ch. 28, 2, p.113).

Grandgousier's own subjects are compensated for war damage ('les feist rembourcer de tous leurs interests', ch. 51, 2, p.187); of course no damage had been caused in Picrochole's territory, where there had been no fighting. Grandgousier's officers are rewarded with 'chasteaulx et terres' (2, p.188), but from his own possessions, not from conquered land. Even Picrochole's army is paid for its services, 'chascun pour troys moys' (ch. 50, 2, p.185), and sent home with a safe-conduct, while Grandgousier's is sent into winter quarters, 'hyverner en leurs stations' (ch. 51, 2, p.187). This is a prudent provision to avoid the disorder which might follow victory; it was the practice of impecunious commanders to let their disbanded army find its own pay in and around the town they happened to be in, and this had been the origin of the gangs of thieves and brigands infesting France at the end of the Hundred Years' War.

The war-criminals are punished, and indeed without trial; but their responsibility had been heavy, and their labour (not stated to be unpaid or for life) is to be turned to the end most useful in Rabelais's eyes: 'Aultre mal ne leurs feist Gargantua, sinon qu'il les ordonna pour tirer les presses à son imprimerie, laquelle il avoit nouvellement instituee' (51, 2, pp.186-87). In the Italian wars the habit had grown up of using all prisoners-of-war indiscriminately for slave-labour; the Swiss preferred not to take prisoners at all, but to butcher the defeated on the spot. Again, Rabelais's detailed suggestions are much in advance of the practice of his time.

But his imagination has taken fire, and sky-rockets beyond the practicalities of post-war reconstruction, in each of his books.

The horizons in *Pantagruel* continually widen. From a comparatively, indeed literally, restricted childhood (ch. 4), the hero proceeds to his tour of the French provinces (5-6). In Paris his intellectual development is broadened and deepened, equally through reading, dispute, friendship and the love-affair briefly mentioned in chapters 23-24. The French setting is ripped apart by his intercontinental voyage to Utopia and the warfare there. From death in battle Epistemon brings back a report of an underworld as big as this world or bigger, containing 'plus de cent millions' of *verollez* (ch. 30, *2*, p.370) and reversing earthly ranks and fortunes; and Alcofribas finds in Pantagruel's mouth yet another world, 'plus de xxv royaulmes habitez' (ch. 32, *2*, p.381), where it is similarly true that 'la moytié du monde ne sçait comment l'autre vit' (*2*, p.380).

According to Lefranc (*1*, III, pp.xlvii-li), supported by Lote (*33*, p.215), Epistemon's raising from the dead is a parody of New Testament miracles, proving that 'Rabelais ... ne croit guère au miracle évangélique et par là-même au christianisme'. Busson is more cautious in his revised edition of *Le Rationalisme* (*13*, p.164): 'Si l'on conteste que Rabelais ait voulu parodier ces textes — ce qu'au reste, je ne prétends pas — il me semble qu'il est difficile de ne pas voir dans l'ensemble de la scène — paroles et gestes — un souvenir au moins inconscient des scènes évangéliques.' Febvre and Screech see little or nothing taken consciously from the New Testament: 'no echoes of the scriptural account' (*41*, p.97); 'les différences éclatent' (*23*, p.229). Numerous similar 'resurrections' or 'healings', in mediaeval epic and romance and even in the *Aeneid*, are traced by Febvre, P.V. Baker (*ER*, XIV (1977), pp.47-57) and Tetel (*46*, p.40; see also p.133 on the style of the chapter). One may add that Rabelais gives an early pointer to epic sources in the lament over Epistemon, 'le plus parfaict des hommes', and in Pantagruel's death-wish, 'il se voulut tuer soy-mesmes' (*2*, p.366), both cast in forms traditional since the *Iliad* (XVIII, lines 32-34), the *Aeneid* (XI, lines 161-63) and the *Chanson de Roland* (ed. Whitehead, Oxford, 1947, lines 2888 and 2929). The detail of the parody, according to Febvre, Antonioli (*6*, pp.144-50) and Carol Clark (*15*, p.96), is aimed against medical, magical and mountebank practice, and popular credulity about them. Antonioli admits that the question of miracle is raised, but more (as Auerbach agrees in *Mimesis*, Bern, 1946, ch. XI) the disturbing of received ideas.

Febvre, however, might rather have called it just a received disturbing of ideas. Rabelais is simply inviting us to pretend that, in the world of fantasy to which he has transported us, death is not a final or serious matter, any more than it was for Snow-White or might have been for Eurydice. In that world, Epistemon's comment that things are not so bad as we think ('si mal que vous penseriez', *2*, p.367) has a wider application. All one risks if one cuts the throat of a giant is a little scratching on the face, 'quelque peu au visaige' (*2*, p.365). Death is merely a rather worse wound, a 'solution de continuité' (ch. 15, *2*, p.297), which can be cured by proper surgical attention. What one needs after it, like Pantagruel after battle, is a good drink, 'un voirre d'un grand villain vin blanc' (*2*, p.367). So it is in the world of fantasy — which yet has its underlying realities. Rabelais, the friar turned doctor, may well be saying that death is less to be feared than his patients tend to think.

Similarly Epistemon's reassuring 'nouvelles des diables et des damnez' (ch. 30, title) are ninety per cent harmless fantasy with ten per cent of real implications. Though Lefranc sees 'le même scepticisme caustique' and 'à l'égard de la papauté, une intention exceptionnellement agressive' (*1*, III, p.1), Febvre again sees little to shock ('un "Dialogue des Morts" fantaisiste et sommaire', *23*, p.253) and Screech picks out only the hits at Charlemagne's peers and the legendary French king Pharamond (*41*, p.97; see also C. Camproux, *Studi Francesi*, XVI (1962), pp.19-30, and E.B. Williams, *EC*, (1963), pp.63-67).

Lucian, Rabelais's source, directed his satire 'Menippus' chiefly against those whose riches, high rank or misguided philosophy had led them to pride: Fortune changes all costumes, Death levels all men, and for Lucian only Socrates and Diogenes remain what they were on earth. Pride is not explicitly mentioned by Rabelais; his list of *damnez*, which grows from edition to edition, includes conquerors and tyrants, but also some who merely lived in the era before Christ or ranked high in later ages, the innocent Lucretia and Hortensia and 'tous les chevaliers de la Table Ronde'. There is seriousness in the pillorying of seven popes, but no attack on the Papacy; Rabelais has not picked popes at random to be condemned simply for being popes. If, as seems probable, he means Julius II, Alexander VI, Sixtus IV, Callistus III and Urban VI, together with Boniface VIII and Nicholas III whom he identifies precisely, all seven were guilty, and publicly known to be guilty, on most or all of the charges of unscrupulousness, nepotism, despotism

and militarism. Into a well-known list of tyrants and aggressors
Rabelais has infiltrated popes who would have been generally
agreed, even by orthodox Catholics of his time, to have been
aggressive and tyrannous.

Though there are a few slight traces of the chronological
succession of the rulers of Rome, the order of the *damnez* in general
is purely associative, or even random and careless, Achilles and
Artaxerxes appearing twice. Punishments consist in humiliation,
being forced into a low-class state of life or occupation; especially
one offering a witty contrast (Demosthenes, to be seen in the
Prologue to *Gargantua* as 'spending more on oil than on wine',
becomes a 'vigneron'), or one with some appropriateness to the
culprit's name ('Piso, paisant') or to his character (Julius Caesar and
Cnaeus Pompeius, who fought famous naval battles, become
'guoildronneurs de navires'). Those who are promoted to be 'gros
seigneurs' in hell (2, p.371) include Lucian's Diogenes, but also
figures who simply held charm for Rabelais, the fictional Fierabras
and Pathelin, and the poet Villon. To make another poet, Jean
Lemaire, into a pope may or may not be a compliment; see
Stephens's argument in *45, passim*, that much of *Pantagruel* parodies
prose works by Lemaire. What Epistemon's hell shows is above all a
carnivalesque reversal of ranks as seen by Bakhtin (*8*) and well
summed up by Williams: the retribution and reversal of status are in
accordance with the Gospel of St Luke, and Epistemon's resurrection
is a mere 'device used by Rabelais' to make this point (*EC*, (1963),
p.67).

In chapters 32 and 33 Rabelais's casual inconsistencies about
Pantagruel's size reach their climax, partly to glorify his hero, mostly
to amuse his reader by making increasingly enormous spoof-
demands on his credulity. (Gargantua's varying size produces similar
paradoxes, but Rabelais glides over them even more casually.)
Pantagruel continues to chat on easy terms with human companions
and (ch. 32) with the narrator himself; yet the giant Loup Garou and
Pantagruel appear in chapter 29 to be equally matched. In Loup
Garou's country are found burdock-leaves the size of a bridge-arch
(ch. 32, 2, p.378); but by that point Pantagruel can stretch out his

tongue 'seulement à demy' for two leagues. The narrator can enter
his mouth without being noticed (ib.), and eleven cleaners can be
swallowed 'comme pillules' (ch. 33, 2, p.383). Donald Frame (*24*,
pp.147-48), followed by Michaël Baraz (*9*, pp.119-20), makes an
entertaining attempt at calculating, to scale, these variations. Chapter
33, where Antonioli (*6*, pp.152-53) sees initial realism developing
into fantasy, explores Pantagruel's digestive system with a clever
simultaneous use of Rabelais's medical, topographical, classical and
practical knowledge, and touches of satire against academic
disputers and refined or would-be refined ladies. The explorations of
chapter 32 interweave much more subtle implications and shifts of
level.

The 'world in Pantagruel's mouth' (on which see Auerbach, loc.
cit., p.68 above; *6*, pp.153-56; *36*, pp.119-22 and *37*, pp.147-50) is a
well-established world, fertile and beautiful, perhaps more so than
our own, perhaps even a preliminary sketch for Theleme: the single
tooth which contains 'les plus beaulx lieux du monde, beaulx grands
jeux de paulme, belles galeries, belles praries ...' (2, p.380)
foreshadows the 'belles gualeries ... les jeux de paulme et ... le grand
parc' of *Gargantua* 55 (2, p.198). The inhabitants are 'christians,
gens de bien' (*Pantagruel* 32, 2, p.379), simple, friendly and
hospitable; but they have limitations and faults like our own, and
suffer from the dangers and obligations natural to their situation.
Rabelais pretends to support the accuracy of Alcofribas's observa-
tions by his usual tongue-in-cheek reasoning. It is possible that
pigeons live in Pantagruel's mouth, for they enter when he yawns; it
is natural that plague should rage there when he has eaten garlic; it is
not only natural but necessary that cabbages should grow there, for
peasants must earn a living, 'ne pouvons estre tous riches' (2, p.378).

As for the brigands who haunt Pantagruel's back teeth — here
is the sting of Rabelais's satire — their existence is explained by
frontier hostility: the senators of 'deçà' take for granted the
wickedness of the 'gens de delà ... mal vivans et brigans de nature'
(2, p.380); the 'gens de delà' are presumably hostile for parallel
reasons. Auerbach complains (in the translation of W. Trask, New
York, 1957) that the 'theme of the discovery of a new world' with its

'revolutionary force which shakes the established order' is left undeveloped by Rabelais, who is 'paralyzed' by the alternative theme 'everything just as at home'. But that is to assume that to 'shake the established order' is in itself better than to criticize eternal human psychology. When Alcofribas says that 'la moytié du monde ne sçait comment l'autre vit' (2, p.380), he is saying both 'Open your mind to unsuspected possibilities' and 'Open your eyes to your own faults'. Rabelais is again using material supplied by Lucian, whose so-called 'True History' features a country in the mouth of a huge whale, with quarrelsome tribes and a farmer's boy ready to converse. But Lucian does not have Rabelais's conversation with the mouth's owner, after which we are left wondering on what level of reality we are, and whether Alcofribas has suddenly expanded in size to mirror the expansion of his experience.

The final chapter of *Pantagruel*, 34, is richer than its brevity suggests (see *41*, pp.102 and 116-17). Rabelais is simultaneously parodying mountebanks' accumulations of wonderful promises never to be fulfilled, Lucian's similar promise in the last sentence of the 'True History', and himself, since the statement that 'les registres de mon cerveau sont quelque peu brouillez' (2, p.385) undermines all he has said and is saying. He has no intention of carrying out his programme of relating 'comment Panurge fut marié ... et comment Pantagruel trouva la pierre philosophale ... comment il espousa la fille du roy de Inde ... comment il combatit contre les diables ... et comment il visita les regions de la lune ...' (though Lefranc, *1*, III, pp.xxxviii-xxxix and *Les Navigations de Pantagruel*, Paris, 1905, produced a rather flimsy argument that in a way Rabelais's third and fourth Books kept to the essentials of the programme). The details offered are so obviously far from being 'toutes veritables' (2, ib.) as to discredit all Rabelais's previous assertions of truth-telling. Yet the abrupt end of the first version of the chapter, 'Ce sont beaux textes d'evangilles en françoys. Bonsoir, Messieurs. Pardonnate my, et ne pensez pas tant à mes faultes que vous ne pensez bien es vostres', has the same sting in its tail as chapter 32, the same warning against unconscious prejudice.

Later editions fill out the chapter and continue it till it doubles in length. The second authorized edition, still in 1533, adds the clause about Panurge, ten words more about the philosopher's stone, and the reference to Proserpine, popularly identified as the wife of Lucifer. More importantly, in and from 1534 the chapter goes on to a violent attack ostensibly on the Sarab(a)ites, an extinct class of disorderly fourth-century monks, 'gens ... qui regardent par un pertuys', which could simply mean people who eavesdrop at chinks in a wall. Between the lines, however, can be read an unmistakeable attack on the cowled censors at the Sorbonne, who had criticized or perhaps even considered censoring the 1533 *Pantagruel* (see Febvre, *23*, pp.107-09, and Screech, *41*, pp.102 and 111-12). Evidently 'Rabelais was sufficiently well protected not to have to worry' (*41*, p.112); the attack remains even after the cautious revisions of 1542, when only the words 'beaux textes d'evangilles en françoys' disappear. It scarifies the hypocrites who pose as pious ascetics but 'live as Bacchanals', burn heretics in sulphur and spend their time — all their time, says Rabelais redoubling the insult — reading works such as his to injure the writers — and Rabelais pours out a stream of virulent variations on the word 'articulant', 'producing indictments for heresy', all echoing the word *cul* as if dismissing the critics with an obscene gesture, which the parallel with peasant scavengers reinforces. Condensed content, vivid vocabulary and a style rich in figures strengthen the assault.

Yet Rabelais interrupts his tirade with the two lines which sum up his ideal of life, 'estre bons Pantagruelistes (c'est à dire vivre en paix, joye, santé, faisans tousjours grande chere)' (*2*, p.387). The enjoyment of life and the tolerant friendliness which we saw reigning in Gargantua's childhood and in Pantagruel's attachment to Panurge are to extend into the lives of all those ready to enjoy Pantagruel's adventures and follow his example. Still more, they will reign in the Utopia of which Rabelais dreams at the end of *Gargantua*.

The reward bestowed on Frère Jean (ch. 52) is an abbey founded jointly by Gargantua and himself. Some critics incline to treat the Abbaye de Theleme as if founded by Jean alone, as a mere

anti-monastic joke; thus for Lebègue ' Thélème est le rêve d'un ...
moine besoigneux ... la société de riches oisifs qu'il imagine ne
présente guère qu'un trait original: le régime anarchique' (*Rabelais*,
Tübingen, 1952, p.7; cf. Desonay, *FR*, p.94, and Vachon, *47*, p.119).
We have seen how Jean is the opposite of typical monks (p.50
above); where they, according to Gargantua, are unpopular,
unwanted in good society and unsuited to it, 'il est honeste, joyeux,
deliberé, bon compaignon ...' (ch. 40, 2, p.153). But Jean's qualities,
and Gargantua's appreciation of them, show themselves in more
positive and constructive ways than chapter 52's elimination of the
obvious and minor attributes of monasteries, walls, clocks and bells,
or even its final reversal of the three basic principles of Catholic
monasticism, where it replaces chastity by marriage, poverty by
riches and obedience by freedom.

Some critics treat the Abbaye as if founded alone by an
enlightened Gargantua, to be the ideal socio-political, religious or
educational community; for Rigolot (*36*, p.81) 'ce ne sont certes pas
les plans du moine qui ont été mis en oeuvre', for Beaujour (*10*,
pp.89-106) it is an absolute monarchy, for Krailsheimer (*28*, p.186) a
Platonist 'set-piece'. It is demonstrably not an educational institution,
'un établissement mixte d'internat pour adolescents' (Demerson, *21*,
p.98). Desonay (*FR*, p.95, followed, e.g., by Frame, *24*, pp.42-43)
complains that 'le texte nous apprend que "les femmes y estoient
repceues depuis dix jusques à quinze ans, les hommes depuis douze
jusques à dix et huict". Or rien dans la suite n'indique que l'on aurait
affaire à des adolescents.' But it was not the practice of sixteenth-
century institutions to specify a leaving-age (see *7*, *passim*). The
ages specified by Rabelais are the maximum and minimum for entry
as a permanent member of the community (as distinct from the
visitors or temporary residents welcomed in ch. 54).

Such members are described throughout as 'hommes' et
'dames', terms which might on occasion be applied to adolescents but
would be unnatural if Theleme received adolescents exclusively.
Members may stay as long as they wish; it is usual to marry on
leaving (ch. 57, 2, p.205) but not necessarily to leave on marrying
('là honorablement on peult estre marié', ch. 52, 2, p.190). No

instruction within Theleme is mentioned; it is assumed that entrants have already received a basic education, as their very age implies; though no doubt they continue their own studies with the help of the excellent libraries and other facilities listed in chapters 53 and 55, and perhaps continue one another's education in the Platonic fashion. Theleme offers a way of living according to the principles of a Renaissance education already begun; but clearly the subject of education is no longer in the forefront of Rabelais's mind.

The subject of religion, however, clearly is so. Gargantua's old Catholic education was replaced not by a merely secular one but by one with a subtle Reformed colouring; similarly, Theleme is not a mere lay parody of a Catholic monastery. The words 'religion' (in the sense of 'convent') and 'abbaye' recur frequently; the 'Inscription' of chapter 54 denounces 'hypocrites, bigotz' in its first line, and in its penultimate stanza welcomes Evangelical preachers, sandwiched between 'nobles chevaliers' and 'dames de hault paraige'; members observe 'les festes et dimanches' (ch. 56, 2, p.201), study Hebrew books (ch. 53, 2, p.193) and have each a private chapel (ch. 53, 2, p.192. For 'chapelle' to mean 'kitchen', according to the ingenious suggestion of Marichal, *ER*, V (1964), pp.69-78, it would need to be shown not merely that that usage was common but that it would be the first, in the absence of contra-indications, to come to readers' minds.) The absence of a minster church, however, is surely deliberate. Just as Theleme replaces chastity — seen as sexual abstinence — not merely by marriage but by full enjoyment of the society of the opposite sex, so it replaces poverty by what the child Gargantua's wealth meant to him (see p.27 above), full enjoyment of all that the Renaissance had made available or could ideally make available in the way of both material and mental riches. And the latter would include, as they included for the re-educated Gargantua, the riches of Reformed Christianity.

The name of Theleme gallicizes a Greek word meaning the will.[18] Rabelais may or may not have been aware of the word's exact

[18] See F. Nykrog, *Revue d'hist. litt. de la France*, LXV (1965), pp.385-97; M. Françon, *BARD*, II, 5 (1966), pp.149-50; Florence Weinberg, *The Wine*

classical and New Testament nuances; he must surely have intended it in the same sense as *vouloir* in the Abbaye's basic rule, 'FAY CE QUE VOULDRAS' (ch. 57, 2, p.204), enunciated in still more profound opposition than before to the monastic principles listed at the end of chapter 52. Febvre (*23*, pp.338-39) traces this precept to Erasmus, and Screech (*41*, p.190) to Cicero; but it appears rather that Rabelais is abbreviating a famous phrase of St Augustine's, 'Dilige et fac quod vis', 'Love and do what you like' (*Tractatus in Epistolam Joannis* ... VII, iv; ed. Migne, 1861, vol. 35, col. 2033; ed. and tr. Paul Agaësse, Paris, 1961, pp.328-29; cf. *39*, I, p.71 and *17*, p.121).

In its wider context this maxim implies, according to E. Gilson (*Introduction à l'étude de saint Augustin*, Paris, 1929, pp.174-75), that, once one is in a true relationship with God, one's desires will automatically accord with His will, and it will be safe to follow them. In its narrower context, according to Agaësse (pp.80-81), it counsels a tactful approach to one's fellow-men: 'Dans le développement où elle s'insère, il n'est pas directement question de l'amour de Dieu, mais uniquement de l'amour fraternel ... Pour libérer l'homme du mal, il n'y a pas de gestes préformés, de méthodes infaillibles: il faut aimer. Selon les circonstances, on devra se taire ou parler, reprendre ou pardonner, user de rigueur ou de patience. C'est précisément la charité qui inspirera l'attitude à adopter.'

Whether adopting either interpretation or both, Rabelais leaves unexpressed the first part of the precept, the necessary precondition of the second. Does he think it unnecessary, or does he think that it goes without saying? More likely the latter, as did contemporary Catholic prayer-books mentioned by Screech (*41*, p.190). It is Picrochole who claims, and is condemned and punished for claiming, the unconditional right to do as he likes, the 'droict de bienseance' which results in 'excès non tolerables à personnes liberes' (ch. 29, 2, p.115). In fact, Rabelais's own precondition appears in the comment which follows immediately on 'FAY CE QUE VOULDRAS', 'parce que gens liberes, bien nez, bien instruictz, conversans en

---

and the Will, Detroit, 1972, pp.124-30; and especially Screech, *41*, pp.187-94.

compaignies honnestes, ont par nature un instinct et aguillon, qui tousjours les poulse à faictz vertueux et retire de vice, lequel ilz nommoient honneur.'

Is this to say that man is naturally good, contradicting the Christian doctrine of the Fall? And if so, is Rabelais also contradicting Grandgousier, who said in chapter 29 that Picrochole's free will and judgment 'ne peult estre que meschant sy par grâce divine n'est continuellement guidé'? Rabelais is not so incautious; no more so than St Augustine, whose thought on this point is explained by Gilson (op. cit., p.190) as follows: 'c'est lui [Dieu] qui garde à l'homme déchu le pouvoir d'accomplir des actions vertueuses quelconques; c'est donc de lui que vient en général à l'homme tout bon usage du libre arbitre; laissé à lui-même, l'homme ne posséderait en propre que le pouvoir de mal faire, le mensonge et le péché.' The rule of Theleme applies not to natural man 'laissé à lui-même', like Picrochole 'laissé au gouvernail de son franc arbitre et propre sens', but to the 'gens liberes', free-born, living in freedom, but also enjoying inner freedom of mind and spirit, freedom from sin; 'bien nez', well-born, but also well-endowed by nature, like Eudemon (see p.40 above), and born again, born of God (John III, 3 and I John III, 9); 'bien instruictz' like the re-educated Gargantua, including his evangelical education; and 'conversans en compaignies honnestes' like that of Gargantua and his friends, but unlike that of Picrochole (ch. 33). The Thelemites' minds, unlike Picrochole's, are open to divine grace (cf. *31*, p.402). What they call honour is what Screech calls synderesis, 'that aspect of moral judgment and persuasion in the soul of man which, although weakened at the Fall, was not obliterated ... a basic orientation of the will towards the good' (*41*, pp.191-92).

Inspired by this and by mutual affection, the joint founders of Theleme and its inhabitants welcome all others of either sex who are prepared to live as 'gentilz compaignons' in the spirit of 'le sainct Evangile' (ch. 54, 2, p.196); they exclude only those who by their bigotry, greed, jealousy or trouble-making exclude love. Screech is right that 'this is the abbey of total freedom' (*41*, p.190; cf. *9*, ch. VII); but Rabelais does not mean it to be a 'somewhat chilling

concept' (*41*, ib.). It is out of friendly loving sympathy that the
Thelemites dress alike (ch. 56), occupy themselves together and pair
off (ch. 57), and that the valets, ladies' maids and other workers
listed in that chapter offer their special talents to the community.
That this is the key to Rabelais's thought is also the view of
Krailsheimer: ' The various definitions of Pantagruelism stress the
duty to love (though the word is not actually used) one another as
well as one's duty to desire God's will... In word and deed Pantagruel
is the living embodiment of *caritas*'; '"Foy formée de charité" est la
grande règle de toutes les règles. Elle explique toute la morale de
Rabelais.' (*28*, p.307, and *29*, p.63).

The racy humour of Frère Jean is not frozen out from Theleme.
It glimmers perhaps in the idea of women's voluntarily adopting a
uniform (ch. 56); probably in the impossible dimensions of the
Abbaye (Clouzot's note in *1*, II, p.406, is that 'les 9332 chambres ...
n'auraient pas eu un mètre chacune de largeur'); and certainly in the
last of the phrases describing the sculpture of the Graces who
'gettoient l'eau par les mamelles, bouche, aureilles, yeulx, et aultres
ouvertures du corps' (ch. 55, *2*, p.198; see *47*, pp.117-22 and *9*,
pp.255 ff.) Just as Catholics have always been able to mingle deep
faith, serious reasoning, high mysticism and jocularity, so, as we
have seen all along, Rabelais firmly believes that a similar mixture
should be permitted to Christians of the Reformation. This belief he
can hold concurrently with his awareness of the gravity and peril of
the conflict already engaging them.

In the very foundations of the Abbaye, according to chapters
57-58, lies a large plate of bronze inscribed with an 'enigma', on the
meaning of which Gargantua and Frère Jean amusingly disagree. A
minor enigma is how far the poem is Rabelais's own work; it is to be
found with variants (but again with the possibility of a double
meaning) in the *Œuvres poétiques* of Mellin de Saint-Gelais
(Lyons, Antoine de Harcy, 1574); but so are other pieces which may
or may not be Mellin's. Studies of the poem and the problems
involved include those of E.V. Telle (*FR*, pp.104-19), R.L. Frautschi
(*French Studies*, XVII (1963), pp.331-40), Rigolot (*36*, pp.95-98),
Screech (*41*, pp.195-206), Costa (*17*, pp.122-24) and George

Sutherland (*RG*, pp.13-38) who lists several of Screech's earlier treatments of the topic. Either Rabelais wrote the poem himself and was later plagiarized, or he took it or most of it from Mellin or some other writer because it suited purposes and attitudes that were his independently. In the present context, it is those purposes and attitudes which matter.

The poem describes competition and struggle, followed by victory and happy rest for those who have persevered. According to Gargantua, what is described is the persecution of Evangelical Christians, in the service of the 'maintien de verité divine' (ch. 58, 2, p.209). According to Frère Jean, in a reply somewhat expanded in 1542,what is described is simply a game of tennis, outdoor or more probably indoor, not unlike the modern squash. Yet squash is one more way, like the games, songs and banquets enjoyed from end to end of both *Pantagruel* and *Gargantua*, of finding pleasure among good company. Both Gargantua and Frère Jean are right. Theleme, like Gargantua's second education, like Pantagruel's and Gargantua's attitude to friendship, like their terms of peace, is inspired simultaneously by a Reformed Christianity and by Pantagruelism.

8. Consequences

None of Rabelais's books (except perhaps the *Cinquiesme Livre*, if it is his) can be said to have a conclusion; at least they had consequences, within their own worlds, in their author's life and in the minds of his public. The *Tiers Livre* has little to do with the programme outlined in *Pantagruel* 34 (see p.72 above); after reopening the subjects of war, colonization and use of economic resources, it passes to the question whether Panurge should marry and, if so, whether it will be a success, to which Rabelais seems to answer that only Panurge can choose and that no one can predict Panurge's or any future. The *Quart Livre* tells the story, still more fragmented and mysteriously symbolic, of a quest for an oracle, 'le mot de la Dive Bouteille' (III, ch. 47, 2, p.594), which Panurge is prepared to take as definitive — a story which breaks off unexpectedly in a burst of laughter shared by Pantagruel and Panurge. A year after publishing this, Rabelais died (probably between mid-January and mid-March 1553, according to J. Dupèbe, *ER*, XVIII (1985), pp.175-76). The posthumously published *Cinquiesme Livre*, probably composed on the basis of unrevised drafts left by Rabelais, finishes the quest in a way which may or may not be true to Rabelais's intentions.[19]

It would be an oversimplification to say that Rabelais was persecuted for his promulgation of a gospel of love. However, the widespread misunderstandings of his general intentions have been traced by Marcel de Grève (*ER*, III (1961)), and the precise facts of

[19] The controversy as to the status of the *Cinquiesme Livre* has raged throughout this century; the latest substantial contributions are those of G.A. Petrossian (*ER*, XIII (1976), pp.1-64), R.M. Berrong (*Studi Francesi*, XXIII (1979), pp.299-308, and *ER*, XV (1979), pp.145-59), M. Huchon (*ER*, XVI (1981)) and Guy Demerson (*21*, pp.303-39).

his 'condemnations by the Sorbonne' by Francis Higman (*Censorship and the Sorbonne ... 1520-1551*, Geneva (Droz), 1979). At least one member of the Sorbonne pronounced *Pantagruel* to be 'obscene' in October 1533. In February 1535 Rabelais thought it appropriate to leave his Lyons hospital abruptly and to spend nearly a year in Rome, among other concerns obtaining the Pope's absolution for his 'apostasy' (see p.9 above). The 1542 editions of *Pantagruel* and *Gargantua*, and the *Tiers Livre* and *Quart Livre*, were condemned almost immediately after they appeared. By 1552 even Calvin was saying that 'outrecuidance diabolique' had led Rabelais into 'aveuglement' (*ER*, III (1961), p.77).

Yet even in that year Rabelais could say,

> Je suys, moiennant un peu de Pantagruelisme (vous entendez que c'est certaine gayeté d'esprit conficte en mespris des choses fortuites), sain et degourt [joyeux]; prest à boire, si voulez. Me demandez vous pourquoy, gens de bien? Response irrefragable: tel est le vouloir du tresbon, tresgrand Dieu, onquel je acquiesce, au quel je obtempere, duquel je revere la sacrosaincte parolle de bonnes nouvelles, c'est l'Evangile ...

(*Quart Livre*, Prologue of 1552, 2, II, pp.11-12)

He has always had readers who have appreciated his unique blend of friendliness, common sense, joviality and piety, and who, from Montaigne and Molière to James Joyce and Ionesco, have learnt from his style, his ideas and his wisdom. Even clichés such as 'Rabelaisian laughter' and 'gargantuan appetite', as they are now casually employed, may imply coarseness and extravagance but recognize the absence of malice and selfishness. Those willing to study Rabelais more deeply are able to reach a fuller understanding of the welcome he extends to the whole of life and to all who are willing to join in that welcome.

Select Bibliography

EDITIONS

1. *Œuvres de François Rabelais*, édition critique publiée par Abel Lefranc [etc.], Paris (Champion), 6 vols, 1912-. Vols I and II, *Gargantua*, 1912-13. Vols III and IV, *Pantagruel*, 1922.
2. *Rabelais, Œuvres complètes*, introduction, notes, bibliographie et relevé de variantes par Pierre Jourda, Paris (Garnier), 2 vols, 1962.
3. *François Rabelais, Pantagruel*, édition critique sur le texte original par Verdun-L. Saulnier, Geneva (Droz), Paris (Minard) (T.L.F.), 1959.
4. *François Rabelais, Gargantua*, ... édition critique ... par Ruth Calder, avec introduction par M.A. Screech, Geneva (Droz), Paris (Minard) (T.L.F.), 1970.
5. (Anon.) *Les Grandes et Inestimables Cronicques: du grant et enorme geant Gargantua* [etc.] ... [s.l.] 1532. Facsimile published by S. de Ricci in *RER*, VIII (1910), pp.57-92.

CRITICAL WORKS

6. Antonioli, Roland, *Rabelais et la médecine , Geneva (ER*, XII), 1976.
7. Ariès, Philippe, *L'Enfant et la vie familiale sous l'ancien régime*, Paris (Plon), 1960. (Mentions Rabelais only once, but valuable for background.)
8. Bakhtin, Mikhail, *Tvorchestvo Fransua Rable*, Moscow, 1965; tr. by A. Robel as *L'Œuvre de François Rabelais et la culture populaire au Moyen Age et sous la Renaissance*, Paris (Gallimard), 1970; tr. by H. Iswolsky as *Rabelais and his World*, Bloomington (Indiana UP), 1984.
9. Baraz, Michaël, *Rabelais et la joie de la liberté*, Paris (Corti), 1983.
10. Beaujour, Michel, *Le Jeu de Rabelais*, Paris (L'Herne), 1969.
11. Berlioz, Marc, *Rabelais restitué*, Paris (Didier), Vol. I, 1979; Vol. II, 1985.
12. Brault, G.J., 'Ung Abysme de Science', *BHR*, XXVIII (1966), pp.615-32.

13. Busson, Henri, *Le Rationalisme dans la littérature française de la Renaissance (1533-1601)*, Paris (Vrin), 1957.

14. ——, 'Science sans conscience', *HR*, VII (1940), pp.238-40.

15. Clark, Carol, *The Vulgar Rabelais*, Glasgow (Pressgang), 1984.

16. Coleman, Dorothy G., *Rabelais: a critical study in prose fiction*, Cambridge (CUP), 1971.

17. Costa, Dennis, *Irenic Apocalypse: some uses of apocalyptic in Dante, Petrarch and Rabelais*, Saratoga (Anma Libri), 1981.

18. Defaux, Gérard, *Pantagruel et les sophistes*, The Hague (Nijhoff), 1973.

19. ——, *Le Curieux, le glorieux et la sagesse du monde dans la première moitié du seizième siècle*, Lexington (French Forum), 1980.

20. Demerson, Guy, 'Tradition rhétorique et création littéraire chez Rabelais', *Études de Lettres*, IV, 2 (1984).

21. ——, *Rabelais*, Paris (Balland, Coll. Phares), 1986.

22. Duval, Edwin M., 'Interpretation and the "Doctrine absconce" of Rabelais's Prologue to *Gargantua*', *ER*, XVIII (1985), pp.1-17.

23. Febvre, Lucien, *Le Problème de l'incroyance au seizième siècle: la religion de Rabelais*, Paris (Albin Michel), 1942.

24. Frame, Donald M., *François Rabelais: a study*, New York (Harcourt Brace Jovanovich), 1977.

25. Glauser, Alfred, *Rabelais créateur*, Paris (Nizet), 1946.

26. Gray, Floyd, *Rabelais et l'écriture*, Paris (Nizet), 1974.

27. Jourda, Pierre, *Le Gargantua de Rabelais*, Paris (S.F.E.L.T.), 1948.

28. Krailsheimer, Alban, *Rabelais and the Franciscans*, Oxford (OUP), 1963.

29. ——, *Rabelais*, Bruges (Desclée de Brouwer), 1967.

30. La Charité, Raymond, *Recreation, Reflection and Re-creation: perspectives on Rabelais's Pantagruel*, Lexington (French Forum), 1980.

31. Larmat, Jean, *Le Moyen Age dans le Gargantua de Rabelais*, Nice (Faculté des Lettres), 1973.

32. Lewis, John, 'Towards a chronology of the "Chroniques gargantuines"', *ER*, XVIII (1985), pp.83-101.

33. Lote, Georges, *La Vie et l'œuvre de François Rabelais*, Aix-en-Provence (Universite d'Aix-Marseille), 1938.

34. Plattard, Jean, *L' Œuvre de Rabelais (sources, invention et composition)*. Paris (Champion), 1910.

35. ——, *La Vie de Rabelais*, Paris (Van Oest), 1928.

36. Rigolot, François, *Les Langages de Rabelais*, Geneva (*ER*, X), 1972.

37. ——, *Le Texte de la Renaissance des Rhétoriqueurs à Montaigne*, Geneva (Droz), 1982.

38. Rocher, Gregory de, *Rabelais's Laughers and Joubert's 'Traité du ris'*, Alabama (University of Alabama Press), 1979.

39. Saulnier, Verdun-L., *Rabelais*, Paris (Société d'Édition d'Enseignement Supérieur), 2 vols, 1982-83.
40. ——, 'Dix années d'études sur Rabelais', *BHR*, XI (1949), pp.105-28.
41. Screech, Michael A., *Rabelais*, London (Duckworth), 1979.
42. ——, *L'Evangélisme de Rabelais*, Geneva (*ER*, II), 1959.
43. Spitzer, Leo, 'Le prétendu réalisme de Rabelais', *Modern Philology*, XXXVII (1939-40), pp.139-50.
44. ——, 'Rabelais et les "rabelaisants"', *Studi Francesi*, IV (1960), pp.401-23.
45. Stephens, Walter, *Giants in Those Days: folklore, ancient history, and nationalism*, Lincoln and London (University of Nebraska Press), 1989.
46. Tetel, Marcel, *Étude sur le comique de Rabelais*, Florence (Olschki), 1964.
47. Vachon, G.-A., *Rabelais tel quel*, Montreal (Presses de l'Univ. de Montréal), 1977.
48. Villey, Pierre, *Marot et Rabelais*, Paris (Champion), 1923.

COLLECTIVE AND SERIAL PUBLICATIONS *(with abbreviations used)*

BARD *Bulletin de l'Association des Amis de Rabelais et de la Devinière*, Tours, 1951-.

BHR *Bibliothèque d'Humanisme et Renaissance*, Paris (later Geneva), 1941-.

EC *L'Esprit Créateur*, Minneapolis, 1961-. Special numbers on Rabelais, III, ii (Summer 1963); XXI, i (Spring 1981).

ER *Études Rabelaisiennes*, Geneva, 1956-.

FR *François Rabelais*, ouvrage publié pour le quatrième centenaire de sa mort, Geneva (Droz), 1953.

HR *Humanisme et Renaissance*, Paris, 1934-1940.

RER *Revue des Études Rabelaisiennes*, Paris, 1903-1912.

RG *Rabelais in Glasgow*, proceedings of the colloquium held at the University of Glasgow in December 1983, ed. James A. Coleman and Christine M. Scollen-Jimack, Glasgow (University of Glasgow), 1984.

RIB *Rabelais's Incomparable Book: essays on his art*, ed. Raymond La Charité, Lexington (French Forum), 1986.

RSS *Revue du Seizième Siècle*, Paris, 1913-1933.

CRITICAL GUIDES TO FRENCH TEXTS

edited by
Roger Little, Wolfgang van Emden, David Williams